MW00514607

A Parent's Guide™ to
Washington, D.C.
Adam T. Lass & Judith Mahoney Pasternak

parent's guide press
Los Angeles, CA
www.pgpress.com

A Parent's Guide™ to
Washington, D.C.

Written by Adam T. Lass and Judith Mahoney Pasternak

Text and Maps © Mars Publishing 2002

Cover design by Michael Duggan

Cover photos
Adam T. Lass (Library of Congress, Father & Son, Washington Monument in the Mall, The National Mall, Union Station, Elephant)
J. McGuire (Jefferson Memorial, Washington Monument & Flags, Washington Monument at Sunset, Smithsonian Castle)
Sierra Weir (U.S. Capitol Building, Cherry Trees, Pandas)

Interior Photos © Photographers as noted

ISBN: 1-931199-02-7

© 2002 Mars Publishing, Inc. All rights reserved. No part of this publication may be reproduced, stored in a retrieval system or transmitted in any form by any means electronic, mechanical, photocopying, recording, or otherwise, except for brief extracts for the purpose of review, without written permission of the publisher and copyright holder.

Mars Publishing and the Mars Publishing Logo, Parent's Guide and the Parent's Guide logo are trademarks of Mars Publishing, Inc. The author and Mars Publishing have tried to make the information in this book as accurate as possible. We accept no responsibility for any loss, injury, or inconvenience sustained by anyone using this book.

This book, and all titles in the Parent's Guide series, are available for purposes of fund raising and educational sales to charity drives, fund raisers, parent or teacher organizations, schools, government agencies and corporations at a discount for purchases of more than 10 copies. Persons or organizations wishing to inquire should call Mars Publishing at 1-800-549-6646 or write to us at **sales@marspub.com**.

At the time of publication of this book, all of the information contained within was correct to the best of our knowledge. If you find information in this book that has changed, please contact us. Even better, if you have additional places to recommend, please let us know. Any included submissions to the new edition of this book will get the submitter a by-line in the book and a free copy of any Mars publication.

Please contact us at **parentsguides@marspub.com**

parent's
guide
press

Edwin E. Steussy, CEO and Publisher
Lars Z. Peterson, Editor
Michael P. Duggan, Graphic Artist

PO Box 461730
Los Angeles CA 90046
www.pgpress.com

contents

Authors' Note

This is the first book we've written together. We couldn't have done it without the gracious cooperation of the Washington, DC Convention and Visitors Bureau – or without the endless help and support of our housemates Jessie Gilbard and Brian Pasternak. We also got much-needed help and advice from restaurant guru Lisa Shannon and style adviser Ellen Davidson. Mars' editor Lars Peterson provided help, grace, and patience.

The first-person comments are all by Adam T. Lass unless otherwise specified.

This book is dedicated to Sylvie and Nicole.

Introduction
Why Visit DC?

My Washington is different – way different – from the national capital in the news. It's not a dusty museum of men in suits; it's a green paradise for children crammed with living history and exciting toys.

My kids and I have enjoyed many a blissful Sunday biking and hiking the endless trails of Rock Creek Park. My older daughter Nicole's first real connection with a wild animal occurred during a close encounter with a young sea otter at the National Zoo. But my connection with the city goes further back than that. I was seven when my mom and I, exploring the grounds of the Capitol building, found a half-hidden stone and terra-cotta meditation grotto, complete with its own tiny burbling fountain. Years later, Nicole learned to love that grotto from her earliest childhood. Still later, when she wrote a report on it for grade school, I learned that that quiet shrine and fountain were the work of Frederick Law Olmsted, the same great architect and planner who created New York City's Central Park. (Nicole got an A on the report.)

Introduction

That's why I was so pleased when I got the opportunity to work with my mother, Judith Mahoney Pasternak, to co-write this guide to this city I've grown so fond of since that visit. That's me in the old – though not so old – photos in this introduction. As a longtime resident of the DC metropolitan area and the father of a daughter who grew up here and one who's growing up here now, I have many answers to the question, why bring your kids here? The shortest is that they'll have a wonderful time – and so will you.

Adam, age seven, running up the steps of the Supreme Court

Some of the longer answers are obvious to anyone sensitive to the romance of history. Chosen and designed by our country's constitutional founders, Washington has been defined by the rich pageant of events and fascinating characters who lived in, worked in, visited, and even invaded the nation's capital.

In no other American city can you take your kids for a walk through so much of the nation's past, from before the Declaration of Independence (Georgetown was founded in 1751 and was named after King George III) and the fervent revolutionary days of Washington, Jefferson, Madison, and Hamilton, through the War of 1812, when much of the city including the White House was put to the torch by marauding Brits, and the Civil War (major battles were fought within a stone's throw – and an easy drive – of the capital). Later, every great social movement – veterans', labor, civil rights, women's rights and peace – came here to put its mark on the city, the country, and even the world.

Why Visit DC?

The Most Powerful City in the World

And of course, you can't miss the mystique that pervades the modern city. In the 21st century Washington is not just the nation's capital. It has joined the great cities of the world – perhaps even become the most powerful city in the world. When the President hiccups, the world holds its breath. This is your chance to introduce the kids to the branches of government and halls of power, to see first-hand how your country works, to meet your town's representatives, senators – maybe even see your President up close and personal.

DC also holds a special place in black American history and culture. It was the birthplace and center of operations for such pivotal figures as Revolutionary-era mathematician and engineer Benjamin Banneker, abolitionist firebrand Frederick Douglass, and brilliant composer and musical innovator Duke Ellington. It has played a pivotal role in every aspect of the struggle for black emancipation, empowerment, and self-government. It's the home of one the nation's prominent black colleges, Howard University, and is the only American city that can claim an unbroken line of black mayors.

But Washington is much more than a working city, especially for kids. The best toy box in the world is waiting for them in "The Nation's Attic." The Smithsonian Museum complex, especially the Natural History, American History (formerly the History and Technology), and Air and Space museums are bursting at the seams with the stuff of childhood fantasies: moon rocks and real rocket ships, glistening steam engines and Indy race cars, life-size elephants and larger-than-life dinosaurs your kids can climb on.

Washington is also a capital of the arts, and I mean all the arts. It's got great collections of paintings and sculpture, both historical and modern. It's got stupendous classical performing arts at the Kennedy Center and is one of the founding cities of the blues and jazz.

Introduction

Gorgeous Green Spaces

Culture, history, and museums only go so far when you've got children with the attention span of a gnat. Not to worry; this town's parks can't be beat when it's time to let the kids blow off a little steam. In fact, Washington is Green City, with the most per-capita parkland of any city in the country. In addition to the Mall, it's got two major rivers, the Potomac and the Anacostia, plus Rock Creek Park, the C&O Canal, and, just a short drive away, the thundering majesty of Great Falls.

Adam on the Mall, age 7.

And speaking of short drives, DC is central to a huge range of other prime locations within a few hours of downtown, from the pristine Atlantic beaches of the Eastern Shore and the Chesapeake Bay (the country's largest watershed) to the mountains of the Appalachian Blue Ridge. It's within range of several national parks, including the C&O National Park stretching 184 miles from the city through Maryland and Virginia. And it's an easy drive to Virginia's historical Williamsburg, Charlottesville, and the battlefields of Gettysburg (not to mention Hershey Park, Six Flags, and other major amusement parks).

All in all, DC is a joy for kids – and parents. This town knows how to host families. Almost everything is kid-proof and *free*, the weather is balmy (in the sixties and up for two-thirds of the year), folks are friendly, and the city is relatively easy to understand and navigate. As this book goes to press, Washington is coming out from under the shadow of September 11th and its sequels. Many of the public buildings that were closed have reopened, and the city is once again a great city that's fun to visit and will leave you and your kids with happy memories for years to come.

1 The Basics

How to Use This Book

This chapter provides basic info for getting around DC and staying here, including transit, places to stay, emergency info, and places to eat. Chapter Two lists by category – and alphabetically within categories – more than 200 things to do with kids in Washington: the museums, the monuments, government institutions from the White House to the Bureau of Engraving and Printing (where you can watch money being made!), plus the city's myriad cultural and sports venues, and a run-down of colleges and universities for older children visiting the area. (We cheat a little, twice. The alphabetical list is preceded by a look at the heart of a visitor's Washington, the area from Capitol Hill to the Pentagon, which contains a huge number of museums, memorials and historic sites; also, some of the things are really for grownups, but we try to give hints about what aspects of those the kids might enjoy.) Chapter Three reorganizes that information geographically, describing some of Washington's neighborhoods and some right outside the city limits. Finally, Chapter Four suggests three day trips to nearby history-laden and/or fun-filled locations from Baltimore to Harper's Ferry, West Virginia.

One caveat: at this writing, there are still government buildings that haven't reopened to the public, most notably the White House and the U.S. Capitol. Both of those, of course, are fairly exciting even from the outside and are well worth going *by* even if you can't go *in*. But by the time you read this, you may well be able to visit them, so use the contact information we provide and check ahead.

The Basics

Planes, Trains, and Automobiles: Getting into Town

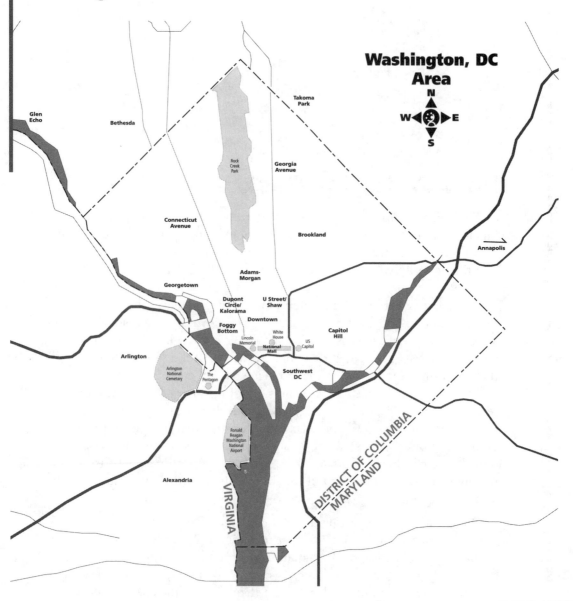

Getting Here

Arriving by Air

Washington Dulles International Airport

45020 Aviation Drive
Sterling, VA 20166
(703) 572-2700
www.mwaa.com/dulles

Washington Dulles International Airport

If you're using public transportation, you can take:

• Washington Flyer Express Bus to the Orange line, Orange line to West Falls Church Metro station, for $8, or to the Downtown Airports Terminal at the Washington Convention Center ($16 one way).

• Super Shuttle door-to-door shared rides ($12-24).

• Taxi (about $40).

Occupying some 11,000 acres in Virginia's Fairfax and Loudon Counties, Dulles is about 26 miles and a half-hour's drive from downtown Washington. In 2000, approximately 20 million people landed or departed from there.

To drive from Dulles to downtown DC, follow signs to I-66 (about 16 miles), then go east on I-66 to Washington.

Ronald Reagan National Airport

Alexandria, VA
(703) 417-8000
www.metwashairports.com/national

Ronald Reagan National Airport

You can get to the city center by:

• Super Shuttle door-to-door shared rides.

• Taxi ($8-17).

• Metro: Yellow, Blue lines to National Airport station.

Reagan National Airport, on the other hand, is virtually inside the city – just across the Potomac in Virginia. Close to 16 million passengers came through it in 2000. (Note: There's no smoking anywhere inside the airport.)

The Basics

BWI Airport

Glen Burnie, MD 21061
(800) IFLY-BWI
www.bwiairport.com

BWI (Baltimore-Washington International) Airport is the farthest from Washington – about 30 miles, or 40 minutes driving time. However, for that very reason, flights into BWI are sometimes cheaper than flights into National or Dulles, so you might want to check it out.

By Rail

Union Station

40 Massachusetts Avenue NE
Washington, DC 20002
(202) 371-9441
www.us.net/dcnrhs/union.htm

You get a double bonus for coming to Washington on the train – not only do you arrive in the heart of the city, you enter into a place that's fun in its own right (see p. 32). The kids will probably want to stop and eat in the food court here before going on – and you might even want to do a little window-shopping in its upscale stores. The station is on the Metro's Red line, so when you're ready to leave you can get to just about any part of the city (except Georgetown) right on the Metro – or, of course, by taxi, if you're overburdened by luggage and kids.

Union Station

By Bus

Trailways-Greyhound Bus Terminal

1005 1st Street NE
Washington, DC 20002
(202) 289-5154
www.greyhound.com

Unlike Union Station, the bus terminal isn't a place you'll be sorry to leave. But it's only five short blocks (on foot or by cab) away from the railroad station, and from there the whole city is accessible (see above).

BWI Airport

You have several options for getting into the city from BWI:

• By car: Follow signs to I-195; I-195 to Baltimore-Washington Parkway South.

• Super Shuttle door-to-door shared rides, $26-$32 for the first passenger, $8 per additional passenger; free for children under 6.

• Amtrak to Washington's Union Station: $21 per adult.

• MARC (the Maryland commuter trains): $5.

Getting Here

Washington's Dream/L'Enfant's Plan: Orientation

Getting around DC is relatively simple, once you know a little of its history. Unlike many older U.S. cities, DC was not the result of organic growth. The 100 square miles that were to constitute the capital were selected by founding father George Washington for the easy commute from his home in nearby Mount Vernon, ceded by Maryland and Virginia, and planned at Washington's behest by his French friend and revolutionary comrade, Pierre L'Enfant.

The design was that of a utopian version of the great capitals of Europe, capturing all of their majesty and grandeur, without the endless meandering lanes and crowded slums that were considered at the time to be an unfortunate hallmark of London, Paris, and Rome. Washington also required L'Enfant to render a capital that could be easily defended from invaders, a reasonable idea considering the military nature of the politics of the time.

The result is a city with an almost perfect alignment to the compass, centered on the Capitol building. It has four sections: NW, NE, SW, and SE. Numbered streets run North-South with 1st Street closest to the Capitol. Lettered streets run East-West, and run through the alphabet four times, first (from the Capitol) as simple letters, than, further away, as one-, two-, and three-syllable names in alphabetical sequence. Finally, the city is crisscrossed diagonally by grand avenues named after the states of the Union (for example, the most famous address in the country, 1600 Pennsylvania Avenue, is at the intersection of Pennsylvania Ave. and 16th Street NW).

The Basics

As will happen when any utopian plan runs head on into the realities of geography and politics, there are a few exceptions to these rules. A quick glance at the map will reveal that the four sections are not truly equal at all. Although the State of Virginia had ceded the city of Alexandria to the District of Columbia, the District ceded it back in 1847, greatly truncating DC's southern quadrants. (Arlington's street naming system still matches L'Enfant's original plan.) There are other minor exceptions caused both by geographical necessity and political reality that we will explore during the course of this book, but once you've got the basics under your belt, the city is relatively easy to get around, on foot and by bike, by bus and subway, and by car. Parking, however, is another story, and we urge visitors to leave cars at home when touring the heart of the city.

About the heart of the city: a large proportion of Washington visitors spend virtually their whole time here in the area bounded on the north and south by Pennsylvania and Independence Avenues and on the west and east by the Potomac River and First Street. The Lincoln Memorial, Constitution Gardens, and National Mall run east from the Potomac until they reach the Capitol; in the center of that green space is the Washington Monument, and north of the monument is the Ellipse and the White House. Much as the authors of this book urge you to see more of Washington than that, we know that you'll want to see that part first.

For More Information

Visitor Information Center

Ronald Reagan Bldg
1300 Pennsylvania Avenue NW
Washington, DC 20004
(202) 347-7201
www.dcchamber.org

This is a fun place to visit. You can ask questions, get tickets, buy gifts and souvenirs, send e-mail "postcards," and take an interactive tour of Washington. (It's run by the DC Chamber of Commerce, 1213 K Street NW, Washington, DC 20005.)

Visitor Information Center

Metro: Blue, Orange lines to Federal Triangle

Hours: Mon-Sat, 8 am - 6 pm.

Cost: Free

More Info

Other resources

Ellipse Visitor Pavilion

15th and E Streets NW, Washington, DC
(202) 208-1631
www.nps.gov/whho

Washington, DC Convention and Visitors Bureau

1212 New York Avenue NW, #600
Washington, DC 20005
(202) 789-7000
www.washington.org

DC Committee to Promote Washington

1212 New York Avenue NW, #200
Washington, DC 20005
(202) 724-5644.

Maryland Office of Tourism Development

217 E. Redwood Street
Baltimore, MD 21201
(800) 634-7386
www.mdisfun.org

Virginia Tourism Corporation

901 E. Byrd Street
Richmond, VA 23219
(800) 321-3244
www.virginia.org

And in an Emergency –

Police or ambulance: dial 911.
For a referral to a doctor or dentist (during business hours): (800) DOCTORS.

Travelers Aid International

1612 K Street NW, #506
Washington, DC 20006
(202) 546-1127

Ellipse Visitor Pavilion

Metro: Blue, Orange lines to McPherson Sq; Red, Blue, Orange lines to Metro Center.

Hours: Daily 8 am - 3 pm; Closed Jan 1, Thanksgiving, Dec 25.

Cost: Free.

The Basics

Getting Around Town

Every town has its own peculiarities when it comes to getting around. Here are a few tips when it comes to Washington's.

First, if you're going to be here more than a few days, or plan on heading outside the downtown area, or figure on doing any serious driving, do yourself a favor and get a couple of good maps. The local favorite for getting around "Beltway Land" (more on that in a moment) is the *ADC Washington DC and Vicinity* map book, available at almost any drug store, supermarket, or 7/11 in the region. It's got a map of the whole area in front, detailed page maps, a blow-up map of the Mall and Downtown complete with cool little pictures of prominent features and landmarks, and a map of the Metro in one handy dandy little book. Honest, there's one of these things in every local's car.

Tip number two: We drive on the right here, contrary to what you may have heard elsewhere.

Now let's talk about the town itself a little. As we mentioned, DC is a 10-mile by 10-mile diamond (if you include Arlington). That diamond is cut into four quadrants: NE, NW, SE, and SW. Those four quadrants are centered on the Capitol Building and are separated by North Capitol Street, South Capitol Street, the Mall, Constitution and Independence Avenues, and East Capitol Street.

All addresses and street numbers (even in Arlington) start from the zero point of the Capitol. Moving east and west, the streets you cross are numbered 1st, 2nd, 3rd etc. Moving north and south, the streets you cross will be lettered: A, B, C, up to W, and then, when you go further, named in alphabetical order with two-syllable names (Adams, Bryant, Channing, etc.), followed still further out by three-syllable street names, also in alpha order (Allison, Buchanan, Crittenden, etc.). The grand avenues named for states usually run diagonally (except for Connecticut and Georgia Avenues, which run due north/south).

At least, that was L'Enfant's intent. The town's rivers and creeks make a lot of this harder to execute on the ground than to draw on paper. (Speaking of creeks, Rock Creek Parkway is a gorgeous way to get uptown, but it's very twisty and has a very strict speed limit. It's also closed to cars on Sundays.)

Getting Around Town

Looking further out, you'll note that the whole town is surrounded by a big interstate highway called the Washington Beltway. On the east side of town, it is designated I95, and on the west, it's I495. Despite any signs you may see while driving on it, it really does go in a big circle. The Beltway is how most of us get around the metropolitan area. You can tell because in rush hour (7 am - 10 am and 4 pm - 7 pm) most of us can be found there, fuming and getting absolutely nowhere. The Washington metropolitan area has some of the worst traffic jams in the country, right up there in the annual studies with New York and Los Angeles. Try to stay away from it you can. If you must travel the Beltway, you reach it from downtown via I295, I395, I66, New York Avenue/Rte 50, the George Washington Parkway (I don't think he slept there), and 16th Street/Georgia Avenue.

The big highways that go past town are I95, I270, and I66. They are for the most part free in Maryland and Virginia, although there are a few tolls out toward Baltimore at the various tunnels and bridges.

Gas is usually about 1.3 times the country's average cost, with any station right by a highway entrance charging a bit more.

Next tip: When parking in DC, read the signs – *all* the signs. Even if there isn't a sign, don't park within 10 feet of a corner. Keep lots of quarters on hand for the meters. DC's parking enforcement crew is legendary; I've seen them tow police cars while their owners were buying donuts. Give serious thought to using the admittedly over-priced private lots. $10 for a couple of hours may be steep, but it beats a $50 ticket hands-down.

And drive carefully. There are lots of police in DC: City police, Park Service police, Capitol Hill police, Protective Services police, and Secret Service police – and they all can and will give you a ticket if they feel like it. (A young friend of mine argued with a Park Cop once, and the cop gave him a court date – in Alaska.)

The Basics

Better Than Driving

The good news is that public transit in Washington is pretty useful – and *very* useful for getting around the central areas, where you'll probably be doing most of your sightseeing. The Metro subway system has five lines – Red, Blue, Orange, Yellow, and Green – and they all interconnect at many central points. Buses go wherever the Metro doesn't. While the Metro may not be as extensive as the New York or Paris systems, the stations are well placed, clean, and safe. Each one features a large map of the system and the various fares required.

Like most subway systems around the world, the Metro is closed at night (specifically, from midnight to 5:30 am on weekdays and to 8 am Saturdays and Sundays), but some buses run all night. The system uses reusable electronic fare cards purchased at dispensing machines in the lobby of each station, with fares ranging from $1.10 to $3.50, depending on the distance. (Most stations have at least one dispensing machine that takes major credit cards.)

Last tip: If you're going to use the subways with any frequency, put at least $5 on the farecard. It saves a lot of grief getting in and out.

For more information, call the Metro at (202) 637-7000 (or look it up at **www.metroopensdoors.com**), or the Washington Metropolitan Transit Authority (WMATA) at (202) 962-1577.

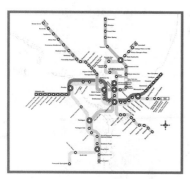

For an expanded map of the Metro, see p. 187.

Where To Stay

Where to Stay

So many hotel rooms – and so few of them priced for families!

Hotels in Washington are a lot more expensive than in other parts of the country – it is the nation's capital, after all – and then (within DC city limits) you have to add on the whopping 14.5% tax. But there are bargains to be found, and some of them are gems. First of all, there are some general principles worth following, and then some suggestions. (We don't have space to list all the possibilities, but Washington's official tourism website, **www.washington.org**, offers many choices in all possible categories.)

The principles:

1. In many hotels and motels, children who share a room with their parents sleep "free" – the price is per room, not per person.

2. Many hotels have special and "promotional" rates going on at various times of the year (after September 11, for instance, many hotels offered "come and be inspired" rates that may still be available to draw visitors to Washington), and some give discounts to AAA and AARP members and holders of various credit cards. Ask. (You may also be able to find hotel deals through online travel services like **Travelocity.com** and **trip.com**.)

3. Away from downtown DC, hotel prices tend to go down. If you're driving to Washington, you can stay in nearby suburbs like Bethesda and still be within Metro reach of downtown. Even within the District, there are pleasant, less expensive places in neighborhoods as famous as Georgetown or as undiscovered as Woodley Park; when you stay in residential areas, you can pay less and be among Washingtonians instead of tourists.

Those principles apply to full-service hotels; if alternatives are a possibility, you can do much better. There's at least one hotel, for instance – right in the heart of downtown – that offers the European-style option of a shared bathroom (shared with other guests, that is) for much less than the price of a room with a private bath. There are also some bed-and-breakfast establishments (although few of them have space for families). And a few DC hotels offer rooms with kitchenettes, letting you prepare some meals at your temporary home instead of paying restaurant bills three times a day.

Finally, for rock-bottom prices, there's hosteling, available to families as well as young people; and, in warm weather, camping. And at the other end of the spectrum, for maximum space, there are a few all-suite hotels that can give you and the kids separate rooms, usually for a price, but in a couple of instances, at rates that will suit the budget-minded.

Here's a sampling of hotels and hotel alternatives offering one or more of the advantages described above.

The Basics

The Big Bargains: Camping and Hostels

Hostelling International

1009 11th Street NW
Washington, DC 20001
(202) 737-2333
www.hiwashingtondc.org

Located right in the heart of downtown Washington (right near the Washington Convention Center, and not far from the Mall and the White House) Hosteling International, associated with the highly reputable American Youth Hostels, offers four-bedded family rooms (without private bath) for the astonishingly low prices of $31 per adult, $11 per child under 12. Guests have the use of a kitchen.

Prince William Forest

Triangle, VA 22172
(703) 221-7181
www.nps.gov/prwi

For families who camp, Prince William Forest, 32 miles south of DC, offers the best bargains of all during the summer months and early fall. We camped there the first time Adam ever came to Washington. It has more facilities now. There are cabins and three separate campgrounds, two run by the National Park Service for tents and RVs, and one privately run for RVs. Prices range from $10 a night for tent sites to $30-$50 per night for four-person to ten-person cabins.

Our tent in Prince William Forest, where we camped the first time Adam came to Washington

There aren't many of the latter, and advance registration is required at most (but not all) of the sites, so write or e-mail ahead. Many of the sites are wheelchair accessible.

Greenbelt Park

Greenbelt, MD 20770
(301) 344-3944
www.nps.gov/gree

A 1,175-acre, 174-site campground 12 miles from Washington, open year-round.

Where To Stay

Budget-Priced Downtown Hotels

Braxton Hotel

1440 Rhode Island Avenue NW
Washington, DC 20005
(202) 232-7800; toll-free (800) 350-5759
www.braxtonhotel.com

A double double-bedded room (for up to four people) with bath from $75 per night, plus free coffee and doughnuts in the morning, all only six blocks from the White House.

Center City Hotel

1201 13th Street NW
Washington, DC 20005
(202) 682-5300
www.centercityhotel.com

The Center City is a little more expensive, from $119 per night for a double-double, but, as its name suggests, it's even closer to the main Washington sights.

Embassy Inn

1627 16th Street NW
Washington, DC 20000
(202) 234-7800

Another hotel in the heart of everything. Rates here can start at $79 a night, including breakfast, plus sherry, champagne, and the *Washington Post* for the grown-ups.

Grand Hyatt Washington

1000 H Street NW
(202) 532-1234; toll-free (800) 233-1234
www.washington.grand.hyatt.com

The Hyatt almost always has special offers available; AAA members get lower rates, as do guests who book on-line. And kids always stay free in their parents' room, while kids under nine eat in the restaurant for half price. Check their website.

The Basics

Hotel Harrington

11th and E Streets NW
Washington, DC 20004
(202) 628-8140; toll-free (800) 424-8532
www.hotel-harrington.com

A family-run hotel near the White House and Capitol, the Harrington has special family rates: two kids stay with two adults starting at $89 per night.

Neighborhood Standbys

Georgetown Suites

1111 30th Street NW/1000 29th Street NW
Washington, DC 20007
(202) 298-7800; toll-free (800) 348-7203
www.georgetownsuites.com

One-bedroom suites with kitchen (and ironing board) from $198 per night, in Washington's famous Georgetown.

Kalorama Guest House at Woodley Park

2700 Cathedral Avenue NW
Washington, DC 20008
(202) 328-0860

Family members in town for special occasions have stayed at this friendly, beautifully furnished bed-and-breakfast near the Washington Zoo. Reasonably priced, but make reservations as far in advance as possible.

If they're full, you can try their other B&B, at Kalorama Park, in Adams Morgan:

Kalorama Guest House at Kalorma Park

1854 Mintwood Place NW
Washington, DC 20009
(202) 667-6369

Jury's Normandy Inn

2118 Wyoming Avenue NW
Washington, DC 20008
(202) 483-1350; toll-free (reservations) (800) 695-8284

Near the charming Dupont Circle neighborhood. From $113 per night – kids sleep free.

Where To Stay

Out in the Suburbs

American Inn of Bethesda

8130 Wisconsin Avenue
Bethesda, MD 20814
(301) 656-9300; toll-free (reservations) (800) 323-7081
www.american-inn.com

A double-double goes for $89, which gets you a 'deluxe' continental breakfast – and free e-mail and Internet connection.

Bethesda Marriott

5151 Pooks Hill Road
Bethesda, MD
(301) 897-9400; toll-free (800) 228-9290
www.marriott.com

Regular rates here can be a little high, but frequent specials can bring the price of a room down to $74 a night. Check the website or call and ask.

The High End

Finally, here's one hotel that gives you everything – for a price.

Holiday Inn on the Hill

415 New Jersey Avenue NW
Washington, DC 20001
(202) 638-1616; toll-free (800) 638-1116
cgoodwin@holinnhill.com; www.sixcontinentshotels.com/holiday-inn

Rates run from $200 per night, but there's a pool and a $5/day supervised children's play program (not always in session, though, so check ahead). Special package deals can bring the rates down.

The Basics

Where to Eat

Washington has thousands of restaurants – a large number of them serving haute cuisine fit for presidents and diplomats, with prices to match. Inexpensive family fare is easiest to find in the fast-food places, but we can do better than Burger King and McDonald's. For those of you who are driving, some of the best food bargains in the DC area are in the suburbs.

Here are a few of our favorites within and outside of the city borders (some are chains and exist both inside DC and in the suburbs; and note that the section on Bethesda, p. 149, has a set of listings all its own). Most (but not quite all) of them are reasonably priced.

Baja Fresh

1333 New Hampshire Avenue NW (Dupont Circle)
Washington, DC 20036
(202) 835-0570

1607 Rockville Pike
Rockville, MD 20852
(301) 770-4339

8515 Fenton Street
Silver Spring, MD 20910
(301) 587-6542

3231 Duke Street
Alexandria, VA 22314
(703) 823-2888
www.bajafresh.com

Baja Fresh is a fast-food taco chain from Los Angeles, but its fresh ingredients and varied menu make the food taste exponentially better than your average Mexican fast food, at comparably low prices. Good chips, salsa bar, and fast service to get those hungry kids fed and back on the road.

Bombay Gaylord

8401 Georgia Avenue
Silver Spring, MD 20912
(301) 565-2528

Bombay Gaylord is an Indian restaurant that's often populated with families, located in downtown Silver Spring. Lunchtime features a popular all-you-can-eat buffet. Favorite items are the shahi paneer (cheese and tomato sauce served with rice), lamb biryani, and the kheer (cardamom rice pudding).

Where To Eat

The Four Seasons

2800 Pennsylvania Avenue NW (Georgetown)
Washington, DC 20007
(202) 342-0444
www.fourseasons.com

Parents looking for peace, quiet, and elegance (and who don't mind paying for them), and kids who dote on the Eloise books, will enjoy starting their day with a fancy breakfast in the dining room of the Four Seasons Hotel in Georgetown. Rock Creek Park, the C&O Canal, and Georgetown are nearby for a post-breakfast stroll. The menu includes American standards, interesting extras such as fresh berries with crème fraîche, and a Japanese breakfast menu.

Guapo's

4515 Wisconsin Avenue NW (Tenley Circle)
Washington, DC 20016
(202) 686-3588

8130 Wisconsin Avenue
Bethesda, MD 20814
(301) 656-0888

Other locations in Gaithersburg, MD; Manassas, VA; and Shirlington, VA.
www.guaposrestaurant.com

Guapo's is a high-energy Mexican restaurant with loud Mexican music, good chips and salsa, cheesy Mexican restaurant decor, and a well-executed menu comprising both the predictable (enchiladas, tacos) and more interesting dishes such as lomo saltado, which is basically beef, onions, peppers, and tomatoes in a savory gravy over a pile of French fries. Excellent margaritas for those accompanying the minors.

The Basics

Hard Times Café

4920 Del Ray Avenue
Bethesda, MD 20814
(301) 951-3300

1404 King Street
Alexandria, VA 22314
(703) 837-0050

3028 Wilson Blvd
Arlington, VA 22201
(703) 528-2233

Other locations throughout the area: Columbia, Rockville, and Laurel, MD; Springfield, Herndon, and Potomac Mills Mall, VA.
www.hardtimes.com

The Hard Times Cafés are chili joints scattered throughout the suburbs, specializing in Texas, Cincinnati, and vegetarian chili. Also featured on the menu are standard kid-friendly items such as chicken tenders and burgers. Good beer list for the grownups, and draft root beer, hot cocoa, and cider for everyone else.

Maggiano's

5333 Wisconsin Avenue NW (Friendship Heights)
Washington, DC 20015
(202) 966-5500
www.maggianos.com

A chain Italian restaurant with decor reminiscent of a Little Italy hangout that doesn't scream "chain restaurant," Maggiano's has good food and a warm family atmosphere. Good pastas, steaks and chops, and other items.

Mark's Kitchen

6921 Laurel Avenue
Takoma Park, MD 20914
(301) 270-1884

A favorite neighborhood hangout for friends and families in vibrant old-town Takoma Park. The half-American, half-Korean menu is strong on vegetarian items (try the grilled tofu platter) but also features spaghetti, burgers, chicken, and the like; you can also choose from a wide variety of juices and smoothies. Nice selection of chocolates by the cash register to stock up on for a busy day.

Where To Eat

Marvelous Market

3217 P Street NW (Georgetown)
Washington, DC 20007
(202) 333-2591

Other locations around the city and inner suburbs.
www.marvelousmarket.com

Marvelous Market is a bakery with branches in various places around the city that specializes in sourdough bread. Features good sandwiches on their fresh bread, upscale grocery-type items such as pasta salads, meatloaf, and sushi, and pastries including dense, fudgey brownies that are exceptional. The Georgetown branch has indoor seating; other locations are carry-out only or have outdoor seating.

My Le

8077 Georgia Avenue
Silver Spring, MD 20910
(301) 588-8385

My Le, an affordable Vietnamese restaurant in downtown Silver Spring, is a favorite among neighborhood people. Families come to savor specialties such as banh xeo (a coconut milk crêpe stuffed with pork and bean sprouts), a highly rated pho and other Vietnamese standards, and an extensive vegetarian menu. My Le's proximity to the Metro and freight-train tracks, about 2 blocks away from the popular outdoor patio, is a big hit for the littlest kids, who have been known to stand up to watch and cheer when a train comes by.

Old Post Office Food Court

1100 Pennsylvania Avenue NW (near the Mall)
Washington, DC 20004
(202) 289-4224
www.oldpostofficedc.com

The Old Post Office, a historic building with clock tower near the Federal Triangle Metro station, is convenient to the museums and has some good food stalls: sandwiches, gyros, Ben & Jerry's ice cream, and Indian food. The masala dosa (a two-foot-long pancake filled with potatoes and onions served with coconut chutney) I ordered recently from the Indian stall drew some fascinated stares from the field-trip kids seated at the next table.

The Basics

Rocklands BBQ

2418 Wisconsin Avenue NW (near Georgetown)
Washington, DC 20007
(202) 333-2558

4000 North Fairfax Dr
Arlington, VA 22203
(703) 528-9663

The Georgetown Rocklands is little more than a lunch counter and carry-out, but the Arlington location is decorated like an old-time gas station and service center and has an outdoor patio. The servings are generous and there's a good beer list for the grownups.

Teaism

800 Connecticut Avenue NW (Downtown)
Washington, DC 20006
(202) 835-2233

2009 R Street NW (Dupont Circle)
Washington, DC 20009
(202) 667-3827

400 8th Street NW (near the Mall)
Washington, DC 20004
(202) 638-6010
www.teaism.com

Teaism opened first in Dupont Circle, featuring an Asian-modern upstairs dining room looking out over the galleries and rowhouses of R Street, and then opened two more branches in neighborhoods farther downtown. Order a ginger limeade or a cup of tea from their extensive selection and select breakfast, lunch, or dinner from their eclectic menu; Asian-influenced items such as bento boxes and ochazuki tea soup are served alongside sandwiches and other Western items. The 8th Street branch serves afternoon tea daily.

Finally, don't forget the **Union Station food court** (see p. 32), a kids' favorite because of the range of choices available.

2

What To Do With Children In Washington

In Chapter One, we covered getting into and around the city and finding a nice place to stay and restaurants that don't get bent out of shape by waist-high customers. Now we get into the good stuff: how to have the time of your life here.

In this chapter, we show you which museums are the most fun (and which one has the best cafeteria). We'll tell you which government buildings are must-sees and which ones are closed to the public. We'll also reveal one of Washington's neatest little treasures, a secret hideaway complete with hidden grotto and waterfall designed by one of the country's greatest landscape architects.

There's more: We've listed some of our favorite getaway spots, beautiful parks with room to run and shout, complete with wonderful picnic spots. We'll show where to find a carousel and a "life-size" dinosaur your kids can climb on. This is also where we'll list Washington's great live performance theaters, especially the ones that cater to young audiences. And we'll tell you how to find where all the local sports team play (and how to get tickets to sold-out games), as well as where the major colleges are.

I first came to this town as a young tourist, a child much like your own. It was so much fun, I never left. Now it's your turn to enjoy one of America's best cities.

What To Do

Down by the River:
From Capitol Hill to the Pentagon

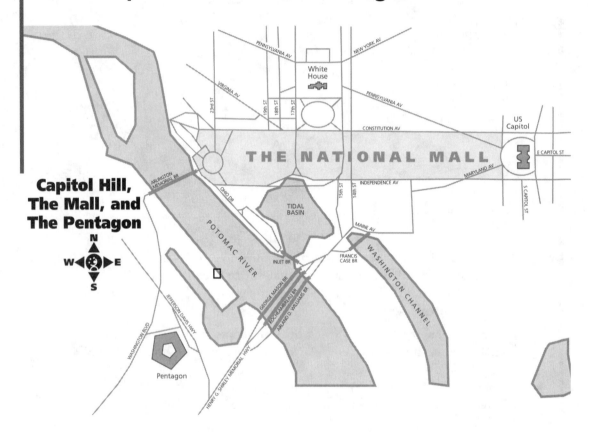

**Capitol Hill,
The Mall, and
The Pentagon**

Down By The River

Capital Children's Museum

800 3rd Street NE
Washington, DC 20002
(202) 675-4120
www.ccm.org

Capital Children's Museum

Metro: Red line to Union Station

Hours: Daily; Labor Day-Easter, 10 am - 5 pm; Easter-Labor Day, 10 am - 6 pm. Closed Thanksgiving, Dec 25 and New Year's Day.

Cost: General, $6; Seniors, $4; Children 2 and under, free.

They call this "the one museum that's all about kids, all the time." It's a no-brainer; you simply must bring your kids here. Many of the other museums in this town do their best to fit children into their mission, with varying degrees of success. The Capital Children's Museum was specifically designed and built with your kids in mind. No mean-looking guards or ancient docents yelling don't run or don't touch. In fact, this place is all about please touch, pull, twist, walk under, and climb on (and some parts look it too, but more about that in a moment).

The CCM is not part of the federally sponsored museum campus. Instead it is housed in a wonderfully funky former convent and home for the poor and aged dating back to 1875, with strange 1960s updates. Located a few short blocks behind Union Station, it's a little off the beaten path, but well worth the short walk.

Visitors enter through a "fantasy garden" – a world just for children – designed by Indian folk artist Nek Chand, with figures made from bits of glass and tile, broken jewelry and even bicycle parts, an invisible harp they can play by waving their hands through thin air, a real city bus and police motorcycle to climb on, and a fire station pole to slide down complete with yellow slickers and real helmets.

The kids can wander through a mirrored maze, learn Pig Latin, or appear on-camera with their favorite cartoon characters (better make that *your* favorite cartoon characters – no fire-breathing Pokemons or broadsword-swinging barbarians here, just Bugs, Daffy, and friends).

What To Do

The Capital Children's Museum has five permanent exhibits and more than a dozen traveling exhibits each year. The newest permanent exhibit is *Brain Teasers*, a hands-on puzzle palace developed by the Oregon Museum of Science and Industry. Five brightly colored areas feature 20 different challenges for young problem-solvers (or old puzzle geeks like me – I could barely drag myself away from them). A special area, *Teasers for Tots*, has been set aside for younger children, with features that invite the museum's youngest patrons to match patterns and shapes, explore motion and color, and strengthen their motor and critical thinking skills.

Other permanent exhibits feature...

- A nearly full-sized **Mexican Village Plaza** complete with a market, kitchen, corner store, log cabin, and public square where you can create crafts to take home and sip delicious Mexican style hot chocolate. While you're there, you can visit a beach on the Yucatan Peninsula and check out a Mayan pyramid.

- A **Chemical Science Center**, where children can investigate whether an "empty" or blown-up balloon is heavier, what conducts electricity, whether hot water is lighter or heavier than cold water, and why 10 + 10 does not always equal 20. The power of air pressure is demonstrated as soda cans crumple, balloons blow up inside flasks, and iced tea brews, all without human help. Interactive demonstrations happen every day. After the demonstrations, children six and older can do experiments in the lab (as long as they are accompanied by an adult.)

- The **Animation Lab** dedicated to Chuck Jones (one of the greatest creative minds of the 20th century – OK, I'm prejudiced, but I grew up watching Road Runner cartoons), with old-fashioned animation machines and a working TV studio where your kids can design a character and create and star in their own cartoon.

- **Cityscape**, where they can slide down a fire pole, drive the metro bus, and surround themselves with an enormous soap bubble! Create your own puppet and make self-portraits with wire, found objects, and paper. (This exhibit is a guaranteed fabulous chance for your kids to get physical and blow off some steam).

- **Japan: Through the Eyes of a Child** whisks visitors to a crowded Japanese street where they can visit an electronics shop, a kimono maker, a local vegetable shop, and a bento counter (where your kids can serve you a genuine Japanese lunch). Children can ride on the Shinkansen bullet train, walk through a Japanese classroom, and check out a modern home, complete with a kitchen, bathroom, and traditional tatami room.

- The **Peace Sculpture**, a unique transformation of violent toys into a universal message of hope and peace. Built in the shape of a child-sized Plexiglas house, the bottom layers are filled with violent toys such as plastic guns, action and wrestling figures, and video games. As the layers rise in height, the violent toys are broken down piece by piece, and non-violent toys, like teddy bears, yo-yos, and building blocks, rise from the recycled remains. This interactive exhibit (messages for peace can be slipped into the sculpture's bottom edge) is the work of six Massachusetts College of Art students.

Down By The River

Visitors spoiled by the high-tech wizardry and deluxe accommodations of the Air and Space Museum and its like may find the Capital Children's Museum a bit run down. Much like a favorite teddy bear, the exhibits are worn at the corners after being loved by millions of kids. The bathrooms are drafty, the halls can get crowded, there's no lunchroom, and the air-conditioning is a little underpowered.

Trust me; your children won't care, and neither will you – you'll be too busy having fun.

Folger Shakespeare Library

201 E. Capitol Street SE
Washington, DC 20003
(202) 544-7077
www.folger.edu

Folger Shakespeare Library

Metro: Orange, Blue lines to Capitol South; Red line to Union Station

Hours: Mon-Sat, 10 am - 4 pm; Closed federal holidays.

Cost: Free.

Folger Library

A Washington curiosity, amid all the government buildings and national museums, is the Folger, the world's largest collection of Shakespeare material – the Bard's own works as well as other Renaissance books and manuscripts. Families with an interest in the stage will find it fascinating, and even relatively young children (eight and up) may be captivated by the Folger's reproduction of an Elizabethan-era theater. (Performances are eclectic, running from chamber music to drama and comedy from a range of time periods.) Curiously, although the grand building was erected in 1932 specifically to house the Folger Library (planned by Henry Clay Folger and Elizabeth Jordan Folger as a "gift to the nation"), no attempt was made to evoke Elizabethan architecture; the building is neo-classical in style and looks like much of the rest of Capitol Hill.

What To Do

Library of Congress

10 First Street SE
Washington, DC 20540
(202) 707-8000
www.loc.gov

Got kids who love to read? Your hometown library is nothing like this one. The Library of Congress holds *17 million* books and more than *95 million* documents (maps – the world's largest collection – photographs, etc.)! It comes as close as anything ever has to housing everything ever printed.

Like the Supreme Court, the Library of Congress lived in the Capitol Building for a long time. By late in the 19th century, however, it was clear that it couldn't go on there – there wasn't room for all the books. (The Library also houses the U.S. Copyright Office.) The extremely lavish main building, the Thomas Jefferson Building, opened in 1897; its 75-foot high Great Hall is one of Washington's more impressive sights. A *Gutenberg Bible* is on permanent display there.

Library of Congress

Metro: Orange and Blue lines to Capitol South

Hours: Mon-Sat, 10 am - 5:30 pm; Closed federal holidays. Public tours of the Jefferson Building available daily (call for information).

Cost: Free.

Library of Congress

The Great Hall is actually what most visitors see, and seeing it may be enough for your family. You can't visit the 532-mile stacks in any case – the Library's primary purpose, after all, is as the research arm of the U.S. Congress – but anyone "over high-school age" can use the collections by getting a user card, and some families may want to investigate their own background in the Genealogy Reading Room.

Down By The River

Supreme Court of United States

1st Street & Maryland Avenue NE
Washington, DC 20543
(202) 479-3211
www.supremecourtus.gov

Supreme Court of United States

Metro: Blue, Orange lines to Capitol South;
Red line to Union Station

Hours: M-F, 9 am - 4:30 pm; Closed federal
holidays.

Cost: Free.

The Supreme Court

A must-see for any family with would-be lawyers or with a general interest in law, justice, or politics, the Supreme Court is the visible representation of the third branch of American government, as significant as the White House or the Capitol.

Despite that, the Court did not have a home of its own until 1935 – for most of its first century and a half, it met in the Capitol Building. Former President and Chief Justice William Howard Taft (the only person ever to serve in both capacities) convinced Congress in 1929 to create "a building of dignity and importance" to house the Court. Architect Cass Gilbert fulfilled that mission with the awesome, football-field size white marble building where the Court now meets, starting each term (as every schoolkid and TV watcher knows) on the first Monday in October. The mammoth male and female sculptures in front present, respectively, the "Guardian or Authority of Law" and the "Contemplation of Justice;" carved at the top of the building is the American ideal, "Equal Justice Under the Law."

From October through about June, visitors can actually watch the Court in session (but the first-come, first-served seating is limited), or can just tour the building, watch a 24-minute film, and eat in the cafeteria.

What To Do

Union Station

40 Massachusetts Avenue NE
Washington, DC 20002
(212) 371-9441
www.unionstationdc.com

You can board a train here for any part of the country – or buy just about anything you or your kids can imagine.

Union Station is all things to all people: the gateway to Washington from 1907 on (and today for some 23 million people a year); one of the city's grandest examples of Beaux-Arts architecture; and now, for better or for worse, a gorgeous high-end shopping mall.

It was built in 1907, during railroading's Golden Age. It was the railroad, after all, that had made one nation out of nearly four dozen states spread across 3,000 miles – and the country was becoming a world power as well. Union Station was the visible incarnation of American optimism, designed by architect Daniel Berman in white granite and gold leaf and covering more ground than any building in the country. Seventeen presidents and innumerable other heads of state have passed through its gleaming corridors.

Union Station	
Metro: Red line to Union Station
Hours: Daily, 24 hours.
Cost: Free.

Union Station

But in the second half of the century, the railroad fell on hard times, eclipsed by air travel as the preferred mode for covering long distances. The nation's grand railroading temples – including Union Station – grew shabby and disreputable. By 1981, leaks in the ceiling had nurtured a deadly fungus throughout the building, and the station was closed and sealed.

There was a savior at hand, however. The new national pastime was shopping, and preservationists around the country were discovering that fading historic sites could be rejuvenated by grafting malls onto them. During the same period, AMTRAK was improving rail travel to compete with airplanes.

Down By The River

Adam T. Lass

The result was a miracle; instead of being bulldozed, Union Station was restored to new life with the addition of more than 130 mostly high-end shops and eating places purveying anything from high fashion to fitness gear to the best chocolates to the best cigars. The food court has everything fast from tacos to spring rolls to ice cream. And if your kids – or you, of course – don't want fast food, there are several higher cuisine options.

Now Union Station hums again with the bustle of thousands of travelers a day, plus thousands more who come here for pleasure. You have to bring the kids here – there's still magic in the railroad aura, and Union Station really is gorgeous. And fun.

U.S. Botanic Garden/Bartholdi Fountain

Maryland Avenue and First Street SW
Washington, DC
www.aoc.gov/USBG/usbg_overview, www.aoc.gov/usbg/bartholdi

U.S. Botanic Garden/ Bartholdi Fountain

Metro: Orange, Blue lines to Federal Center Southwest

Hours: Daily, 10 am - 5 pm.

Cost: Free.

Overdosed on marble corridors and stuffy museum rooms? Hungry for some natural beauty? The lovely two-acre Botanic Garden is the oldest continuously operating botanic garden in the country – but, be warned, not for those with allergies. It boasts a conservatory (you can even enjoy the flowers on a rainy day!), as well as the National Garden, a spectacular collection of American blooms.

Immediately adjacent is the lavish Bartholdi Fountain, designed by Frédéric Auguste Bartholdi, the man who created the Statue of Liberty.

What To Do

U.S. Capitol

Capitol Hill
Washington, DC 20515
(202) 225-6827
www.aoc.gov

There are some places in Washington that your kids will drag you to, and other places where you will have to provide the impetus. Unlike the museums and parks, you may need to push younger kids up the hill to the Capitol Building, but by all means, do it; it's worth it. In fact, they'll probably thank you for it afterwards (and certainly will when they're older).

The U.S. Capitol Building, with its dome and two wings, is one of the most familiar images in Washington. More than any other site in Washington, it is simultaneously an incredible repository of history and art and the working center of the world's most successful democracy.

The Capitol is the only place in the world where your kids can gaze at glorious statues and paintings of our country's founders, and then cross paths with their own hometown's rep-

U.S. Capitol

Metro: Orange, Blue Lines to Capitol South; Red line to Union Station

Hours: Open *for guided tours only*, Mon-Sat; Closed Thanksgiving, Dec 25, New Year's Day.

Cost: Free, but tickets required (first-come, first-served) from East Front Screening Facility (near fountains on East Front Plaza). Note that stringent security measures prohibit not only guns, mace, etc., but "oversize back-packs," cans and bottles (if in doubt, call ahead and ask).

The Capitol Building

resentative as he or she heads for the floor to vote on issues that could directly affect their lives. This is where the rubber hits the road when it comes to governing the country. Few folks realize just how exciting the place can be.

Or how beautiful it is. The building itself was designed to be the ultimate physical symbol of our freedom from the rule of tyrants, the Parthenon and the Pnyx (where the ancient Athenians were the first to try their hand at democracy) rolled into one public shrine to working democracy.

Down By The River

In fact, Greek and Roman temples were the inspiration of the Capitol's neo-classical column-lined galleries, rotundas, and endless marble halls lined with statues of heroes and leaders. That inspiration began to take form in 1793 according to the designs of Dr. William Thornton, the first of ten architects of the Capitol.

The original brick-clad sandstone building was finished for the first time in 1826. The north and south wings – added to house the growing country's equally growing deliberative body – and the new dome were completed in the mid-nineteenth century. The final piece, the East Front, was finished early in the twentieth. (That dome, by the way, contains almost nine million pounds of cast iron.)

For most of our country's life, the Capitol not only housed the offices, committee rooms, and deliberative chambers of both branches of Congress, it also accommodated the Library of Congress until 1897 and the Supreme Court until 1935. (Both the Supreme Court and the Library of Congress are now located only a short walk from the Capitol Building and are also well worth visiting – if the kids have any patience left.)

Now it's "just" where 100 senators and 435 representatives wrangle over the laws that affect every aspect of our daily lives... mostly in public view. In fact, until September 11th, you could walk right into just about any senator or representative's office, a level of freedom that most of the world couldn't even imagine. If you call ahead, you can still usually get an appointment to speak with your own local representative, and some will even get you a flag that flew over the Capitol to take home with you.

Over the years, I've probably been inside the Capitol a dozen times. But I've strolled the grounds countless times, even when I had no intention of going inside. The park-like setting – designed by our country's greatest urban designer, Frederick Law Olmsted – is especially pretty when the Victorian-era gaslights are illuminating it around dusk. Also, several times a year, the National Symphony holds free concerts on the West Lawn, always an enjoyable evening for families. Schedules are available by calling (202) 467-4600.

What To Do

And you won't want to miss one of Washington's most beautiful secret spots. Near the Northwest corner of the grounds, near New Jersey Avenue, Olmsted built a little hidden retreat, called the Summer House, complete with stone benches, a burbling fountain, and a grotto and rock garden. Built of red brick in a fascinating basket-weave pattern, and accessed by a series of elegant classic archways, it was created to offer Congressmen a respite from the sweltering heat of the pre-air-conditioned Capitol. My mom (and co-author) and I first discovered it quite by accident on my first trip to Washington when I was seven. But it is so cleverly hidden, I was unable to locate it for another 15 years, until I stumbled across it again while walking with my older daughter Nicole. I made a point of bringing my mom back the next chance we got, and it's now one of our favorite spots in the city.

On a practical level, you should keep in mind that the Capitol is now a very secure building. All access is through the East entrance, and you and your crew will have to pass through a checkpoint similar to those in airports, so you might want to leave any pocketknives in the car, or at home.

Also, you can expect a bit of a line getting in, so get there early. I generally like to do the Capitol before lunch, while the kids are still fresh, and then grab a bite to eat in one of the fine restaurants on Pennsylvania Avenue or perhaps in one of the nearby museum cafeterias. Better yet, plan ahead and pack a picnic lunch, as the nation's lawn, the National Mall, beckons you at the foot of Capitol Hill.

Adam T. Loss

The Mall

The Mall and Beyond

Adam T. Lass

Adam T. Lass

Adam T. Lass

The Mall

N
W · E
S

The White House

The Ellipse

CONSTITUTION AV

23rd ST
22nd ST
21st ST
20th ST
VIRGINIA AV

Vietnam Veterans Memorial

Constitutional Gardens

Reflecting Pool

Lincoln Memorial

HENRY BACON DR

DANIEL FRENCH DR

Korean War Veterans Memorial

17th ST

MADISON DR

Washington Monument

15th ST

14th ST

JEFFERSON DR

Nat'l Museum of American History

Nat'l Museum of Natural History

Nat'l Gallery of Arts

Smithsonian Institute (Castle)

Freer Gallery

Hirshorn Museum

Nat'l Air & Space Museum

7th ST

4th ST

3rd ST

PENNSYLVANIA AV

2nd ST NW

NEW JERSEY AV

DELAWARE AV

MARYLAND AV

Supreme Court

E CAPITOL ST

US Capitol

1st ST

PENNSYLVANIA AV

MARYLAND AV

S CAPITOL ST

NEW JERSEY AV

INDEPENDENCE AV

ARLINGTON MEMORIAL BRIDGE

Potomac River

OHIO DR

Franklin Delano Roosevelt Memorial

Tidal Basin

Jefferson Memorial

Adam T. Lass

Adam T. Lass

What To Do

National Mall

Between Constitution & Independence Avenues SW
Washington, DC 20002
(202) 485-9880
www.nps.gov/nama

Something tells me it's all happening at the Mall. . . Running from the Washington Monument to the Capitol, this is Visitor's Central, the home of a dozen museums – most of them free, including nine of the Smithsonian Institution's 13 DC branches – spaced out along approximately a mile of green space where the family can picnic and the kids can ride a carousel or romp on grass or around a life-size dinosaur. (If you're there during the winter, they can even ice-skate – see National Gallery, below). It's also where tents are put up for exhibits of every kind; and, finally, it's where some of the nation's largest demonstrations and protests have been held.

The amazing variety of things to do along the Mall has an added bonus for art-loving parents. You can negotiate with the kids – two hours, say, in the Air and Space or Natural History Museum gets you one in the Sackler and Freer Galleries, for instance. It's an especially good bargain because

The National Mall

you'll probably have just as wonderful a time in the Air and Space and Natural History Museums as the kids will. And the free admission means the family can wander in and out of all or any of these as your fancy takes you.

The Mall

The Smithsonian Museums – An Overview

The Smithsonian Institution (**www.si.edu**) facilities in Washington include, on the Mall (and described on the following pages) all of the following:

- Smithsonian Institution Building ("The Castle")
- Arthur M. Sackler Gallery; Arts and Industries Building
- Freer Gallery of Art
- Hirshhorn Museum and Sculpture Garden
- National Air and Space Museum
- National Museum of African Art
- National Museum of American History, Behring Center
- National Museum of Natural History
- International Gallery-S. Dillon Ripley Center.

Smithsonian 'Castle'

J. McGuire, courtesy Washington DC Convention & Tourism Corp

Elsewhere in the city (and described in "Museum City," p. 69):

- Smithsonian American Art Museum
- Anacostia Museum and Center for African American History and Culture
- National Portrait Gallery
- National Postal Museum.

The National Zoological Park is described in "The Great Outdoors," p. 90. And finally, the National Museum of the American Indian will move to Washington this year from its previous home in New York City.

What To Do

Arthur M. Sackler Gallery

1050 Independence Avenue SW
Washington, DC 20560

and

Freer Gallery of Art

Jefferson Drive at 12th Street SW
Washington, DC 20560
(202) 357-4880
www.asia.si.edu

Arthur M. Sackler Gallery and Freer Gallery

Metro: Blue, Orange lines to Smithsonian

Hours: Daily, 10 am - 5:30 pm; Closed Dec 25.

Cost: Free.

This could be one of the places you have to bribe the kids to visit (unless they're particularly interested in things Asian). The Arthur M. Sackler Gallery and the adjacent Freer Gallery constitute the Smithsonian Institution's National Museum of Asian Art. Between the two, they have more than 27,000 works of art from all of Asia, covering the whole span of human history, including paintings, sculptures, bronzes, porcelain vases, and Chinese jade ornaments from the third millennium B.C.E. (The Freer also contains paintings by American artist James McNeil Whistler, who helped arouse Western interest in Eastern art early in the 20th century.)

Arts and Industries Building

900 Jefferson Drive SW
Washington, DC 20560
(202) 357-1300
www.si.edu/ai/

Arts and Industries Building

Metro: Blue, Orange lines to Smithsonian

Hours: Daily, 10 am - 5:30 pm; Closed Dec 25.

Cost: Free.

Two bonuses here: the Mall's carousel is right in front of the Arts and Industries Building – and this is the branch of the Smithsonian with the Discovery Theater for kids.

From this seed grew the giant that is now the Smithsonian Institutions. Originally called the U.S. National Museum, the red brick and sandstone Arts and Industries Building opened in 1881, having been built as a permanent home for objects from the country's Centennial Exposition in Philadelphia in 1876. ("Arts and Industry" was the theme of the Centennial Exposition.) The building was restored in 1976 for the U.S. Bicentennial, but its collections had long since been dispersed to other parts of the Smithsonian. Its chief glories now are its splendid Victorian architecture and the aforementioned Discovery Theater, which features performances for children with live actors, puppets, musicians, and mimes.

The Mall

Hirshhorn Museum and Sculpture Garden

Independence Avenue at 7th Street SW
Washington, DC 20560
(202) 357-2700, (202) 633-8043 (TTY)
http://hirshhorn.si.edu

Hirshhorn Museum and Sculpture Garden

Metro: Green, Yellow, Blue, Orange lines to L'Enfant Plaza

Hours: Daily, 10 am - 5:30 pm; Closed Dec 25. Plaza open 7:30 am - 5:30 pm; Sculpture Garden, 7:30 am - dusk.

Cost: Free.

Hirshorn Sculpture Garden

Another no-brainer for art-loving parents; you get to look at a stunning collection of modern and contemporary sculpture (including Rodin's "The Burghers of Calais") *while the kids run around outdoors*! The Hirshhorn exhibits (indoors and out) works by Degas, Picasso, Käthe Kollwitz, Andy Warhol – in other words, all the modern masters. But for many, the building itself is as exciting as any of sculptures; others hate it. Built in the early 1970s by architect Gordon Bunshaft specifically to house modern art, the Hirshhorn's design is as distinctive as (and architecturally similar to) Frank Lloyd Wright's for New York's Guggenheim Museum. It's also small enough so that you can see much of it in one afternoon, if the kids have the patience for it.

International Gallery

S. Dillon Ripley Center
1100 Jefferson Drive SW
Washington, DC 20560
(202) 357-4282, (202) 357-1729 (TTY)
www.si.edu/ripley

International Gallery

Metro: Orange, Blue lines to Smithsonian

Hours: Daily, 10 am - 5 pm.

Cost: Free.

The International Gallery is a kind of Smithsonian miscellany, hosting an eclectic range of exhibits and programs on subjects ranging from microbes to jazz. It's a small facility, entered from a copper-domed kiosk on the Mall. Since you'll be in the neighborhood anyway, you might as well check out their current exhibit in case it's something you or the kids are particularly interested in.

What To Do

National Air and Space Museum

Independence Avenue at 7th Street SW
Washington, DC 20560
(202) 357-2700
www.nasm.si.edu

Moon rocks. Your kids can touch a real piece of another world here (so can you). And if that doesn't thrill them, they can sit in the rocket that flew there and back, or even design their own spaceship and see it fly to the stars.

The Smithsonian Air and Space Museum features a broad range of exhibits on the history and science of human flight, and houses and displays hundreds of full-sized planes and rockets.

It is the world's most popular museum, with more than ten million visitors a year from hundreds of countries. And it's easy to understand why. Its unique combination of history, science, and technology with enough whiz-bang, biggest, fastest, highest, firsts will thoroughly engage the attention of the most media-jaded 12-year old.

Designed by Gyo Obata to be a spacious marble and steel shrine to human ingenuity and drive, the Air and Space Museum opened on July 1, 1976, as part of the nation's bicentennial celebration. But its collection began a century earlier, with a gift of kites from the Chinese Imperial Commission following the closing of the 1876 Centennial Exposition in Philadelphia.

National Air and Space Museum

Metro: Blue, Orange lines to Smithsonian; or Green, Yellow, Blue, Orange lines to L'Enfant Plaza

Hours: Daily, 10 am - 5:30 pm; Closed Dec 25.

Cost: Free. Admission to show at Albert Einstein Planetarium, $4; admission to Langley IMAX® Theater varies by show. Undergoing renovation through 2001; call or see website for information on closed exhibits. Cafeteria in basement.

National Air and Space Museum

Adam T. Lass

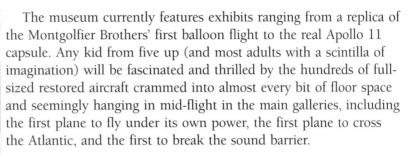

The Mall

The museum currently features exhibits ranging from a replica of the Montgolfier Brothers' first balloon flight to the real Apollo 11 capsule. Any kid from five up (and most adults with a scintilla of imagination) will be fascinated and thrilled by the hundreds of full-sized restored aircraft crammed into almost every bit of floor space and seemingly hanging in mid-flight in the main galleries, including the first plane to fly under its own power, the first plane to cross the Atlantic, and the first to break the sound barrier.

The side halls are filled with informative interactive displays about everything from the science of aerodynamics and orbital mechanics to the original 1960s Enterprise made famous on the TV show *Star Trek* and Luke Skywalker's flight suit from the *Star Wars* movie series.

Still can't get your teenager interested? The Langley IMAX Theatre has larger-than-life thrills to compete with the best amusement parks and mundane movie theaters. And some teens will drool over the muscular WWII-era P-51 Mustang in full battle dress, or the sleek, jet-powered Messerschmitt Me-262 Schwalbe (Swallow).

This museum was made for kids, so you won't hear a lot of "don't touch" here. And the spacious design and bright lighting make for easy and enjoyable viewing. But don't kid yourself; when they say "most popular museum," they are not joking. If you decide to visit during peak season (July-August and spring break) you will be sharing the experience with millions of other families, a manageable but somewhat intense experience. Try to go during the week when crowds are smaller and lines shorter.

What To Do

National Aquarium

Department of Commerce Building, Room B-077
14th Street between Pennsylvania and Constitution Avenues NW
Washington, DC 20230
(202) 482-2825
www.nationalaquarium.com

Sharks, piranhas, alligators – kids can see them here, at the country's oldest public aquarium. Not only can they see them, but at 2 pm every day, they can watch one or another of those predators *being fed* – ooh!

That said, this aquarium can't touch the one in Baltimore (see p. 168). It hasn't changed a lot since it first opened (not in this building) in 1873, and some of the fish look as if they've been swimming around ever since. But it does display some 270 species of fresh- and salt-water critters, and it has the advantage of being around the corner from dozens of other things you want to see – and the price is right.

> **National Aquarium**
>
> Metro: Blue, Orange lines to Federal Triangle; Red, Blue, Orange lines to Metro Center
>
> Hours: Daily, 9 am - 5 pm. (Gift shop open Fridays and weekends only.)
>
> Cost: General, $3; children 2-10, $.75; children under two, free.

National Gallery of Art

Constitution Avenue NW between 3rd and 9th Streets
Washington, DC 20565
(202) 737-4215
www.nga.gov

National Gallery of Art

This is the big one – two buildings, one immense collection, and none of it part of the Smithsonian. A relatively late arrival among the world's major art museums (it opened in 1937), the National Gallery of Art certainly belongs in that club by now. Thousands of paintings and sculptures are housed in its two huge facilities, with pre-20th century art

The Mall

National Gallery of Art

Metro: Orange, Blue lines to Smithsonian; Red line to Judiciary Square

Hours: Mon-Sat, 10 am - 5 pm; Sun, 11 am - 6 pm; Closed New Year's, Dec 25.

Cost: Free.

in the West Wing and modern and contemporary art in the East Wing, designed by I.M. Pei and opened in 1978. There's no way you can see all of it in one visit, so don't try. If you're there in the winter, however, and the kids get antsy, you can give them an ice-skating break in the East Wing's sculpture garden as an alternative to the usual museum-cafeteria break.

National Museum of African Art

950 Independence Avenue SW
Washington, DC 20560
(202) 357-4600, (202) 357-4814 TTY
www.nmafa.si.edu

A treasure trove from throughout Africa, this branch of the Smithsonian is unique in several ways. Its collection covers three millennia of African arts and crafts, including ceramics, jewelry, and miniature ivory animals from Kerma, the chief city of the kingdom the ancient Egyptians (and the Bible) called Kush, and seven centuries' worth of art from Benin in West Africa pre-dating British colonial rule. The museum is also unusual in that its exhibit floors are entirely underground. (That was how room was made for it in 1987 on a Mall that was already crowded with museums and other buildings.) Educational programs for visitors of all ages explore Africa's rich story-telling and musical heritages as well as its visual arts.

National Museum of African Art

Metro: Orange, Blue lines to Smithsonian; or Green, Yellow, Blue, Orange lines to L'Enfant Plaza

Hours: Daily, 10 am - 5:30 pm; Closed Dec 25.

Cost: Free.

What To Do

National Museum of American History

14th St. and Constitution Avenue NW
Washington, DC 20560
(202) 357-2700
www.americanhistory.si.edu

Planes and rockets you saw across the Mall at Air and Space. Classic paintings and modern art abound at the National Galleries. Now it's time for just about anything and everything else that could possibly qualify as "Americana."

While we locals always bring out-of-towners to other, flashier exhibits, this is the one I return to year after year. Its ever-changing collection has never failed to capture my and my daughters' attention, regardless of age. Immense glistening steam locomotives that tower over you, huffing and chuffing as if they're about to plow through the wall, Mario Andretti's '69 Indy-winning winged wonder, Richard Petty's sky-blue hot rod Pontiac that he drove to his two-hundredth victory, and Big Daddy Don Garlit's monstrous drag racing rail.

Sure it's got printing presses, machine shops, light bulbs, clipper ships and farm tractors, Jackie O's dresses, George's wooden teeth, and Theodore Roosevelt's very own stuffed "Teddy" bear. But it's also got wide-screen videos of an Ella Fitzgerald and Duke Ellington duet and Pueblo sacred dances and . . . The temptation to just

**National Museum
of American History**

Metro: Blue, Orange lines to Federal Triangle; Blue, Orange lines to Smithsonian

Hours: Daily, 10 am - 5:30 pm (extended in summer hours); Closed Dec 25.

Cost: Free.

National Museum of American History

The Mall

list exhibits is strong, but however long a list I give you (and the selection here is so strong, so diverse, and so fascinating I could go on for pages and not cover everything your kids can fall in love with in just one visit), it wouldn't begin to convey what this particular museum offers.

Of all the Smithsonian Museums, this one is truly the one that qualifies as the "nation's attic." I must confess that this was my other favorite museum when I was a kid. Sort of the ultimate toy train set, except that some of the engines are bigger than a house. And in its earliest incarnations, it did tend to focus on techie stuff – mostly feats of engineering like trains, ships, bridges, and tunnels.

But now your kids can get up close and personal with a vast array of pure American history, from the flag that inspired Francis Scott Key to jot down our national anthem to star-spangled items like Dorothy's ruby slippers, Archie Bunker's ratty old armchair, and Jobs' and Wozniak's prototype Apple computer. And I do mean up close; there are history and science sections where your kids can get behind the glass and touch the stuff our country is made of.

The sixth museum to open on the national mall, the National Museum of American History first opened to the public in January 1964 as the Museum of History and Technology. The museum's 750,000 square feet house exhibits, workshops, laboratories, offices, libraries, archives, and other support areas along with an auditorium, a bookstore, gift shops, public and staff cafeterias, an ice cream parlor, and a genuine old-style (and still working) post office.

The building, a National Historic Landmark, is also on the National Register of Historic Places, both because of its location and because it was one of the last structures designed by the renowned architectural firm of McKim, Mead, and White.

Entering from the Mall directly into the museum's second floor, you'll find a vast multi-story lobby with maze-like wings on either side chock full of culture and history, like the First Ladies Hall. Far more than inaugural ball gowns, the exhibit also covers the pivotal social and political roles of the nation's presidential spouses (of special interest, Eleanor Roosevelt's December 7, 1941, recorded radio announcement broadcast at a "very serious moment.")

"From Parlor to Politics" details women's struggles for health care, access to higher education and the right to vote, while "Field to Factory" traces the African-American migration from the rural southern fields to northern factories and the impact of that migration on the fabric of American life.

47

What To Do

Enter on Constitution Avenue, and you'll start out on the museum's first floor with a more technological focus. "A Material World" is a complex stew of human-made objects, from bricks to transistor radios as well as the huge machines, tiny dioramas, and endless galleries of ship models mentioned earlier.

For some hands-on fun, I recommend "The Information Age," a jam-packed, interactive exhibit tracing the collecting, organizing, and transmitting of information from the telegraph to the Web, with models of the first transistor, old TVs, and fancy hi-fis (remember when stereo was a big deal?), a factory robot dancing around a car in mid-production, and the Ur-Apple, the very first Apple computer built in a garage by Steve Jobs and Steve Wozniak.

The kids can get a bar-coded brochure at the entrance that they can scan at various stations, where they'll learn how the FBI uses computers to store and retrieve the loops and whorls of their fingerprints; punch in their ZIP code to see what direct marketers think of the neighborhood you live in; and print out a detailed account of their visit.

More interactive exhibits can be found at the museum's hands-on science and history rooms, where docents will guide kids five and up through activities and experiments designed to expand and illuminate exhibits in the rest of the museum.

In the history room, your kids will enjoy mounting the high-wheeler bicycle (straight off the playing cards), cranking a cotton gin, making their own rope, and dozens of other activities, like tapping a telegraph key, sorting

The Mall

mail, running a treadle sewing machine, and rifling through a Colonial-era girl's personal trunk. In fact, this room is so packed with . . . stuff that there's no way your kids will get through it all in the 30 minutes allotted to each group.

The science room has lab-style tables staffed by some of the coolest, well, "power-geeks" this side of Stanford and MIT to help your kids perform experiments that illustrate scientific concepts, as well as tables full of intriguing puzzles, mini-experiments, and even a laser you can aim at a picture of the moon across the room.

Oh, I forgot to mention the museum's top floor, which has the skimpiest selection for kids. Just Judy Garland's ruby slippers from *The Wizard of Oz*, a *Star Trek* phaser, Indiana Jones' slouch hat and leather jacket, and Michael Jordan's Chicago Bulls jersey.

Much like the Natural History and Air and Space museums, the National Museum of American History can get pretty crowded in spring and summer, but offers a delightful day-long respite during the fall and winter. These days, there's always a bit of line to get in while guards check your bags. And while the cafeteria is by far the newest and most pleasant on the mall, with an imaginative and tasty selection, lunch for a family of four can set you back 60 bucks real quick. In warmer weather, I personally prefer a picnic out on the mall.

It's virtually impossible to see everything here, so don't even try. Instead, do what the natives do, and come back year after year. Because no matter their age or interest, there's something here that's guaranteed to make your kids' jaws drop and their eyes sparkle while they learn about their home.

What To Do

National Museum of Natural History

Constitution Avenue at 10th Street NW
Washington, DC 20560
(202) 357-2700
www.mnh.si.edu

National Museum of Natural History

Metro: Blue, Orange lines to Smithsonian or Federal Triangle

Hours: Daily, 10 am - 5:30 pm (extended in summer hours); Closed Dec 25.

Cost: Free.

Butterfly Garden in the Museum of National History

The world's biggest elephant confronts you as you walk in the door, trunk raised in mid-trumpet, as the sound of elephant cries and bird calls fill the air of the gothic four-story central marble and granite rotunda.

This museum has it all: mummies, masks, talons, trunks, hatchets, and haunted gems. Its endless maze of galleries contains some of the coolest stuff the natural world has to offer, including dinosaurs (fossil skeletons, of course, but also some surprisingly lifelike full-size reproductions), whales, birds, frogs, Polynesian canoes, an African village, volcanoes, and a (cursed?) diamond as big as your kid's fist.

Second jewel of the crown of kids' must-see Washington museums, the National Museum of Natural History displays a vast treasure trove of more than 120 million natural and cultural objects that reveal the forces that generate, shape, and sustain natural and cultural diversity.

Modeled after the grand gothic cathedrals of Europe, it first opened its doors to the public in 1910 with a display of Atlas lions from President and adventurer Teddy Roosevelt's latest haul. In addition to its public exhibits and displays, it houses hundreds of researchers and scholars examining every aspect of the natural world and sponsors field expeditions across the face of the globe.

But that's not what's going to turn your kids on. What's going to light up their eyes are *bugs*! In a side hall on the second floor, you'll find the Orkin Insect Zoo, where your youngsters can spend hours peering at live giant beetles, hissing Madagascar cockroaches, and a functioning beehive that connects to the outdoors via a clear Plexiglas tube.

The Mall

Your little naturalists will also want to visit the bird hall, where they can check out a broad array of birds from around the world. And they shouldn't miss the birds of Washington, DC on the ground floor, especially if they think this town is all about stuffed shirts. That's where they'll find an impressive collection of local avians, including golden eagles, bald eagles, and great horned owls. These displays have helped generations of visitors identify local species. Year-round and seasonal residents of the region extending from the Atlantic Ocean to the Allegheny Mountains – hundreds of species in all – are displayed here.

In addition to the mounted dinosaurs, the museum's working fossil lab is a must for budding paleontologists, as are the displays on early life, human evolution, and Ice Age mammals. For kids with an anthropological bent, there's the Asian Cultures, Native Cultures of the Americas, and Pacific Cultures exhibits.

And speaking of "primitive cultures," the Smithsonian is finally attempting to rectify a problem that haunts many of the older natural history museums around the country. For most of the 20th century, these museums demonstrated a markedly patronizing attitude concerning "native" cultures (e.g., arrowheads and topless women in straw dresses here in Natural History, but steam engines and Victorian clothes next door in the American History museum). I highly recommend checking out the museum's new exhibit, African Voices. It brings a new sense of dignity and significance to the exploration of African history and daily life, and its significant influences on American history and culture (not to mention some really cool interactive displays that will knock your kids' socks off).

If your kids are into geology (my older daughter, Nicole, always used to come home from school with backpack-loads of rocks that had caught her eye), they will be thrilled by one of the world's finest collections of gems and minerals, including the gorgeous Hope Diamond, at 42.5 carats the world's largest deep-blue diamond. (The staff steadfastly denies that story about the Hope curse, but revel in the notoriety nonetheless.) And don't forget that volcano!

The museum has benefited in many ways from its recent round of upgrades. It now sports a very nice IMAX theatre, showing features like *Everest* and *Michael Jordan to the Max* in IMAX's usual mind-blowing intensity and now in 3-D as well. Its atrium café is very airy and pleasant, if just a little pricey (a problem with many of the Smithsonian cafeterias), and every bathroom I've been in now has changing tables for the youngest members of your party. And speaking of the carriage class, they do allow strollers, but I recommend using the Constitution Avenue entrance, as the stairs on the mall side are brutal.

What To Do

Smithsonian Institution Building "The Castle"

1000 Jefferson Dr. SW
Washington, DC 20560
(202) 357-2700

The original home of the Smithsonian, built in 1855, the entrancing red sandstone "Castle" now holds the institution's offices and an information center for finding out everything you need to know about all the Smithsonian museums.

Smithsonian Institution Building "The Castle"

Metro: Orange, Blue Lines to Smithsonian

Hours: Daily, 10 am - 5:30pm; Closed Dec 25.

Cost: Free

U.S. Holocaust Memorial Museum

100 Raoul Wallenberg Place SW (across from the Mall)
Washington, DC 20024
(202) 488-0400
www.ushmm.org

Not recommended for young children (under 11), the Holocaust Museum is a profound and moving experience for older kids and adults. You should give it a morning or an afternoon to itself; you won't want to go to anything else immediately afterward, and you will want to be able to sit and talk about what you've seen.

U.S. Holocaust Memorial Museum

Metro: Orange, Blue lines to Smithsonian

Hours: Daily, 10 am - 5:30 pm; Closed Yom Kippur and Dec 25.

Cost: Free, but timed passes are required for the permanent exhibition, "The Holocaust." Get them at the museum or the day before from **www.tickets.com**.

To tell its grim story, the museum uses photographs, films, oral histories, and objects like the possessions of concentration-camp prisoners found when the camps were liberated at the end of the war. The building's architect, James Ingo Freed, visited concentration camps and European ghettoes while he was designing the museum in order to make the structure's design consonant with its intent. The central Hall of Remembrance, which serves as the country's national memorial to the victims of the Third Reich, is a large open space lit by natural light, with epitaphs on the walls and niches for candles visitors can light as personal memorials. The permanent exhibit, "The Holocaust," takes place on all three floors of the building and is meant to be viewed in sequence, beginning with "Nazi Assault" and ending with "The Last Chapter" (covering the end of World War II and the full revelation of the horrors of the Holocaust). The museum has a cafeteria in case you need a break, but the passes are timed to allow you to progress straight through the exhibit.

The Mall

Washington Monument

15th Street and Constitution Avenue NW
Washington, DC 20001
(202) 426-6841
www.nps.gov/wamo

Washington Monument and flags

This was our country's first grand monument to its progenitor, and they didn't want anyone to make any mistake about just how proud of him we are. Trust, me, you won't. This is one bold, proud pile o' marble.

Precisely 555 feet tall, the monument not only defines the Washington skyline, it's also one of the world's tallest freestanding masonry structures – all in all, a pretty cool icon, right up there with the Eiffel Tower and the Empire State Building. To stand there on the hill, looking down at the city or the Lincoln Memorial, while the monument's flags snap in the breeze, gives me a bit of a thrill to this day. But the monument's austere design and magisterial beauty belie the slightly twisted story of how the thing got built.

Congress first came up with the idea in 1833, 34 years after Washington himself passed away. Architect Robert Mills' original proposal included some pretty baroque plans for a whole involved Revolutionary War Memorial. Problem: like so many other new families just starting out, ours was pretty broke, and all we could afford was the centerpiece, a simple stone obelisk.

Washington Monument

Metro: Orange, Blue Lines to Smithsonian

Hours: Fall-winter – daily, 9 am - 5 pm; April-Labor Day – daily, 8 am - midnight; Closed Dec 25.

Cost: Free; timed passes required.

The next thing that happened was this (and this is so – well, so Washingtonian): from 1848 to 1854, they worked like the dickens and had about a third of the monument completed, when political infighting and bureaucratic turf wars ground construction to a halt. For 25 years, red tape and indifference kept it a big stub, until

What To Do

Ulysses Grant spearheaded the drive for the monument's completion at the centennial celebrations in 1876. Construction resumed in 1878 and was completed in 1884, and the structure was dedicated by President Chester A. Arthur the following year.

The catch: the long delay in completion yielded one of the monument's most notable features – it's two different colors. Stones from the quarry in Massachusetts used to consruct the bottom of the monument didn't quite match the stones from Maryland used to finish it. If you squint at the monument on a sunny day, you can see that the marble on the top two-thirds is brighter and pinker than the base. (For years, my dad had me convinced that this discoloration was a result of the famed Johnstown flood, and that the line between the two colors was the high-water line. I tried the trick when my daughter, Nicole, was about the same age and got a lecture on the sheer impossibility of such a thing. Kids!)

Anyhow, they've just completed cleaning it up for the millennium (two years late, but well ahead of schedule compared to the last go-round), and you can go up to the summit in a nice air-conditioned 72-second elevator ride, during which a park ranger describes the construction and design of the building. The view of the city is incomparable. Heck, you can probably see your house – in Albuquerque – from the top. On weekends, the National Park Service offers a special staircase tour; you get to walk down 897 steps and check out the 190-odd memorial stones mounted along the walls, gifts to the memorial from all 50 states, as well as various groups, individuals, and a nation or two.

Free timed-entry tickets are available at the kiosk on the 15th Street side of the monument on a first-come, first-served basis. Or you can cheat and order yours from TicketMaster, (800) 505-5040 for a small fee. Even with a ticket, there will still be a line at the base.

The Mall

A Carousel and a Really Big Dinosaur

Carousel

Finally, two of the biggest smile makers on the Mall aren't museums at all. One is a mid-sized open-air carousel in front of the Smithsonian Castle. The sight of my daughter laughing as she bobs up and down on a gaily painted unicorn immediately wipes away an hour and a half of "Are we done yet?" in the National Gallery.

The other cool camera shot is right across the Mall, in front of the Museum of Natural History: a giant, "life-sized" concrete triceratops statue that your kids can climb right up on. It's the perfect solution for children who have had it up to here with "do not touch."

The grandeur continues past the Washington Monument with the Reflecting Pool leading up to the Lincoln Memorial. This is also where you'll find Maya Lin's moving Vietnam War Memorial (and, for good measure, the Korean War memorial).

What To Do

Lincoln Memorial

West Potomac Park at 23rd Street NW
Washington, DC 20024
(202) 426-6841
www.nps.gov/linc

Adam T. Lass

"Four score and seven years ago our fathers brought forth on this continent, a new nation, conceived in Liberty, and dedicated to the proposition that all men are created equal . . ."

Abraham Lincoln, November 19, 1863

The "Gettysburg Address," etched on the wall of the Lincoln Memorial.

"I have a dream that one day on the red hills of Georgia, the sons of former slaves and the sons of former slave owners will be able to sit down together at the table of brotherhood . . . I have a dream that my four little children will one day live in a nation where they will not be judged by the color of their skin but by the content of their character. I have a dream today . . ."

Rev. Dr. Martin Luther King Jr., August 28, 1963

"I have a dream," delivered at the Lincoln Memorial and etched on the American memory.

The Mall

They're speeches every child in the nation knows. This is where they come to learn more about the man who made the first one – and where the second one was made (to an audience of 250,000, including one of the authors of this book). The Lincoln Memorial is one monument that has seen almost as much history as it commemorates.

Lincoln Memorial

Metro: Orange, Blue lines to Foggy Bottom

Hours: Daily, park ranger in attendance 8 am - midnight; Closed Dec 25.

Cost: Free.

On its walls are inscribed the words of the Gettysburg Address and Lincoln's other unforgettable speech, the Second Inaugural Address. In the center sits sculptor Daniel Chester French's massive, three-times-life-size statue of the 16th president, brooding still over a nation he continues to influence.

Yet the nation had no monument to our 16th president until 1922, when the memorial was finally dedicated. Ground was broken in 1914, but the intervening World War slowed construction.

As if to make up for a half-century of waiting, the Lincoln Memorial is an awe-inspiring structure, its seven-foot diameter columns 44 feet high, the whole building rising 99 feet above the ground. Architect Henry Bacon imagined it as a kind of temple to democracy and designed it along the lines of the Parthenon of ancient Athens, considered the birthplace of democracy. Bacon built a 36-column colonnade around the three-chambered structure and had inscribed at the top of each the name of one of the 36 states that made up the Union at Lincoln's death. The two chambers that flank the statue contain the speeches and murals by artist José Guerin.

In the 80 years since the memorial's dedication, Lincoln's image continues to mark the U.S. collective imagination – so much so that, while other monuments reflect history, this one has shaped it, more than once drawing landmark events that have changed American life.

In 1939, for instance, contralto Marian Anderson was booked to give a concert in Constitution Hall, the performance space of the Daughters of the American Revolution. Then someone at the DAR found out who Anderson was – at that moment, the nation's most prominent black classical music performer – and the DAR canceled the show.

What To Do

The snub scandalized the nation. First Lady Eleanor Roosevelt resigned from the DAR in protest. Secretary of the Interior Harold L. Ickes did more than protest; he found Anderson a better concert site. On Easter Sunday, 75,000 people came to the Lincoln Memorial – the largest crowd that had ever gathered there – to hear Anderson's recital. She opened with "America."

The crowd that heard Marian Anderson sing would be dwarfed 24 years later, on August 28, 1963, when a quarter of a million people came to the March on Washington for Jobs and Freedom. The people lining the Reflecting Pool from the Lincoln Memorial to the Washington Monument could not have known that they were about to hear a speech that would become one of the most celebrated in the nation's history, perhaps second only to the Gettysburg Address.

Franklin Delano Roosevelt Memorial

1850 West Basin Drive SW (south of Lincoln Memorial, near the Cherry Tree Walk)
Washington, DC 20024
(202) 619-7222
www.nps.gov/frde

The monument to the Depression era-World War II President honors FDR himself, First Lady Eleanor Roosevelt (the only First Lady so honored), and the long period through which he led the nation. Its four "chambers" holding sculptures, bas-reliefs, and inscriptions of some of Roosevelt's best-known quotes (such as, "the only thing we have to fear is fear itself") stand for the four times he was elected president. Most older kids should know that FDR was the only person ever elected to the U.S. presidency more than twice, prompting Republicans to pass the 22nd amendment to the Constitution, which limits the presidency to two terms. Two of the statues depict him in a wheelchair – he was our only disabled president – and the entire monument is wheelchair accessible, the first such memorial to be intentionally designed for accessibility.

> **Franklin Delano Roosevelt Memorial**
>
> Metro: Orange, Blue lines to Smithsonian
>
> Hours: Daily; park ranger in attendance 8 am - midnight; bookstore open daily 8 am - 10 pm; restrooms close 11:45 p.m. Closed Dec 25.
>
> Cost: Free.

The Mall

Thomas Jefferson Memorial

Off the National Mall on south side of Tidal Basin
Washington, DC 20024
(202) 426-1844
www.nps.gov/jefm

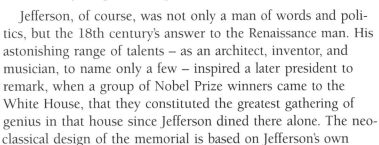

Thomas Jefferson Memorial

Metro: Orange, Blue lines to Smithsonian

Hours, Daily, 8 am - midnight; Closed Dec 25.

Cost: Free.

In 1943, with monuments in place to George Washington and Abraham Lincoln, the nation dedicated this one to the third president and author of the Declaration of Independence. It, too, has walls engraved with the words of the man it honors – in this case, words long since engraved in the pages of American history and the very shape of our government.

Jefferson Memorial

Jefferson, of course, was not only a man of words and politics, but the 18th century's answer to the Renaissance man. His astonishing range of talents – as an architect, inventor, and musician, to name only a few – inspired a later president to remark, when a group of Nobel Prize winners came to the White House, that they constituted the greatest gathering of genius in that house since Jefferson dined there alone. The neoclassical design of the memorial is based on Jefferson's own design for the rotundas of the University of Virginia (which Jefferson in turn had based on the Pantheon in Rome).

Korean Veterans Memorial

National Mall at Independence Avenue (near the Lincoln Memorial)
Washington, DC 20024
(202) 619-7222
www.nps.gov/kwvm

Korean Veterans Memorial

Metro: Orange, Blue lines to Foggy Bottom

Hours: Daily, 8 am - midnight.

Cost: Free.

Early in the 1990s, Congress decided that the Vietnam Veterans Memorial (see next page) could be perceived as a slight to the one-and-a-half million Armed Forces members who served in Korea and authorized this monument, which sits just southeast of the Lincoln Memorial. Nineteen statues, a wall etched with 2,400 anonymous faces, and a Pool of Remembrance constitute the major elements of the memorial, which tends to be a quieter and more reflective spot than the more controversial Vietnam monument.

What To Do

Vietnam Veterans Memorial

Constitution Avenue and Henry Bacon Drive NW
Washington, DC 20001
(202) 634-1568
www.nps.gov/vive

Vietnam Veterans Memorial

Metro: Orange, Blue lines to Smithsonian

Hours: Daily, 24 hours; park ranger on site 8 am - midnight.

Cost: Free.

The scars of the war that divided the United States as bitterly in the 20th century as the Civil War had in the 19th were still fresh when the Vietnam Veterans Memorial was dedicated in 1982. The monument is still visited every year by the parents, widows, and children of the 58,000-plus Americans who died in Vietnam, whose names are inscribed on the memorial in the order they fell. Many visitors to the monument remember the million-plus dead of Vietnam, as well.

Ironically, the design of the stark black V-shaped wall that constitutes the memorial made the career of the young architect Maya Lin, who was still a

student when she submitted her design for consideration in 1981. The simplicity of the wall, however, angered some Vietnam veterans groups, and a representational statue of three soldiers was subsequently placed at the entrance to the memorial.

The names of the dead are listed in alphabetical order at both entrances to the monument.

The Mall

North of the Mall: The Ellipse and the White House

Zero Milestone

North Ellipse
Washington, DC
http://pubs.usgs.gov/gip/stones/

Zero Milestone

Metro: Blue and Orange lines to Farragut W. or McPherson Square; Blue, Orange, Red, lines to Metro Center

Hours: Daily, 24/7.

Cost: Free.

This is one of those things that kids love the idea of; Washington designer Pierre L'Enfant imagined a column a mile east of the Capitol "from which all distances of place through the continent were to be calculated." It didn't quite work out that way, but all the national highways that pass through DC are measured from this granite marker. It's right near the White House, so you can stop and see it in passing.

White House

1600 Pennsylvania Avenue NW
Washington, DC 20502
(202) 456-2200

J. McGuire, courtesy Washington DC Convention & Tourism Corp

What To Do

It's the White House – the *White House*!

Even glimpsed from across the street and through a fence (and for the time being that may be the only way you'll be able to see it), no child – nor any adult – can fail to be awed by the sheer power this white-pillared building radiates. Decisions made within those walls have shaped our lives and those of much of the rest of the world. For the 201 years from 1800 to 2001, the White House was the world's only open-to-the-public (except in wartime) residence of an elected chief executive and came to symbolize an idealized relationship between government and governed.

So even if your family can't actually go inside, the kids (and you) will probably want to look at the White House from Lafayette Park or Pennsylvania Avenue. If they're school-age, they're probably already familiar with the basics of its history.

That history began in 1790, when the new Congress declared the (as-yet-unborn) city on the Potomac as the nation's capital and President George Washington and his head city planner, the Frenchman Pierre L'Enfant, chose a site close to the center to be the president's home. After several architects had submitted proposals, Irish-born James Hoban was chosen to build it. He modeled it on the white stone manors of Ireland; as the red brick buildings of the period grew up around it, it came to be called the "White House," although its official designation was the "President's Palace." It would be renamed the Executive Mansion before Theodore Roosevelt accepted "White House" as its official name in 1901.

Now, after 212 years and numerous renovations, the White House has 132 rooms (in sharp contrast to the approximately 600 rooms of England's Buckingham Palace), 32 bathrooms, 412 doors and 147 windows, 28 fireplaces, seven staircases and three elevators. It employs five chefs and can feed dinner to 140 guests and takes 570 gallons of white exterior paint at every repainting. And it has a tennis court, a pool, a movie theater, and a bowling alley.

White House

Visitor Office recorded information line
(202) 456-7041

**www.nps.gov/whho,
www.whitehouse.gov, www.whitehouse-history.org**

Metro: Blue and Orange lines to Farragut W. or McPherson Square; Blue, Orange, Red lines to Metro Center

Hours: At this writing, the White House is open to the public **only for pre-reserved (through a member of Congress) tours by school groups.** The White House Visitor Center (see p. 64), however, remains open to the public. Call the number above for updates.

Cost: Free.

The Mall

And if all this information and a glimpse from the outside doesn't satisfy your family, you should stop by the White House Visitor Center (see p. 64), where you can at least take a virtual tour.

White House events of significance

1792: Construction starts, with architect James Hoban in charge (despite fire and massive renovations, the present exterior walls are still the white stone walls Hoban built). African-Americans – slave and free – make up a large proportion of the brick makers, quarry workers, and carpenters working on the construction.

1800: John and Abigail Adams move in.

1805: Thomas Jefferson, the first president to occupy the White House for his entire term of office, holds the first inaugural open house. It was also Jefferson who proposed the extensions that became the East and West Wings.

1814: During the War of 1812, British soldiers burn the Capitol and the White House, destroying much of the White House. It is evacuated, but First Lady Dolly Madison oversees the removal (and thus preservation) of already-famous historic objects including a portrait of Washington.

1817: Reconstruction under Hoban's supervision completed; Madisons move back in.

1822: Pennsylvania Avenue constructed north of White House.

1829: During Andrew Jackson's inaugural, the 20,000-strong crowd of guests overflows the White House and is served drinks on the lawns.

1865: Paul Jennings, once a slave belonging to President James Madison, publishes the first White House memoir by a former resident, *Colored Man's Reminiscences of James Madison*.

1885: Grover Cleveland takes the inaugural open house out of the White House and transforms it into today's inaugural parade.

1889: The first woman appears on the White House payroll.

1902: The noted architectural firm McKim, Mead, and White ('White' was pre-eminent American architect Stanford White) renovates the White House, building the extension later known as the West Wing. The Executive offices moved to the West Wing under President Theodore Roosevelt.

1909: Oval Office constructed in the West Wing.

1925: President Calvin Coolidge broadcasts nationally (over radio) from the White House for the first time.

1929: With President and First Lady Herbert and Lou Hoover in residence, another fire damages parts of the building.

1948-52: President and Harry and First Lady Bess Truman move to Blair House for the duration of another renovation.

1979: Egyptian President Anwar Sadat and Israeli Prime Minister Yitzhak Rabin celebrate Egypt-Israel peace treaty in the White House.

1999: Much of the television-watching public learns more about how the Executive works when *The West Wing* becomes one of the most popular prime-time dramatic series ever.

What To Do

White House Visitor Center

U.S. Dept. of Commerce Bldg.
1450 Pennsylvania Avenue NW
Washington, DC 20004
(202) 208-1631; toll-free (800) 717-1450
www.nps.gov/whho, www.whitehouse.gov.

White House Visitor Center

Metro: Blue, Orange, Red lines to Metro Center

Hours: Daily, 7:30 am - 4 pm; Closed New Year's, Thanksgiving, Dec 25.

Cost: Free.

Before September 11, 2001, this was where visitors got their (free) tickets to tour the White House, and if the Executive Mansion ever re-opens to the public, it presumably will be again. Meanwhile, this is where you supplement your view from the outside with exhibits on White House architecture, furniture, First Families, etc., along with a 30-minute video. There are no food facilities here.

Federal Triangle

Bureau of Engraving & Printing
U.S. Treasury Dept.

14th & C Streets SW
Washington, DC 20228
(202) 874-3019; reservations (202) 874-2330, toll-free (866) 874-2330
www.bep.treas.gov

**Bureau of Engraving & Printing
U.S. Treasury Dept.**

Metro: Blue, Orange lines to Smithsonian

Hours: M-F, 9 am - 2 pm; Closed federal holidays.

Cost: Free, but reservations required, which must be made two to ten days in advance.

Some kids (and some parents?) will definitely think this is the coolest place in Washington. This is where you can *watch money being printed* – from blank sheets to "wallet-ready bills"! (You can also acquire the "residue" of destroyed currency by applying to the Department of the Treasury, but be warned. You have to tell the feds what you want it for, and the rules governing its reuse are encyclopedic.)

You can also find out here everything you ever wanted to know about money – and things you never dreamed of, like the rules mentioned above governing the disposal of "used" bills.

The BEP designs, engraves, and prints all U.S. paper currency. Established in 1862, it was then located in the basement of the Treasury building and had a staff of six. The Bureau moved to this site in 1914 and opened a second site (not open to the public) in Ft. Worth, Texas, in 1991.

The Mall

FBI Building

935 Pennsylvania Avenue NW
Washington, DC 20035
(202) 324-3447
www.fbi.gov

FBI Building

Metro: Red, Blue, Orange lines to
Metro Center or Green, Yellow, Red
lines to Gallery Place-Chinatown

Hours: Open for school groups
only at this writing, but due to re-
open to the public in spring 2002.

Cost: Free.

When I was growing up, some kids wanted to be astronauts, some were always cowboys, and some kids wanted to be G-men, and shout "FBI." The Federal Bureau of Investigation's place in the firmament has taken a few knocks following the lurid revelations of the '60s and '70s, not to mention more recent crises like the betrayal to Russia of vital Bureau secrets by veteran agent Robert Hansen and the "misplacing" of evidence at the McVeigh Trial.

But there is no denying that J. Edgar Hoover's finest continue to hold the imagination of today's kids, assisted by modern media torch-bearers like the *X-Files*' Agents Scully and Mulder. For a certain kind of kid, a look at the FBI's headquarters is going to be the highlight of a trip to Washington. Romance and reality.

Believe it or not, J. Edgar Hoover was not the first G-man, although he is credited with popularizing the term. The modern FBI actually has its roots in a small working force of special agents appointed in 1908 by Attorney General Charles Bonaparte to act as the investigative arm of the Justice Department.

The present headquarters were built in 1974 to house the rapidly growing force of special agents as well as the enormous support facilities required by modern criminal detection methods. Any kid with an eye on a job at headquarters should keep in mind that while the FBI may have 11,400 Special Agents busting bad guys around the world, it's the 16,000 support personnel working hard day and night at computer terminals and lab benches who do much of the real work of solving mysteries and catching felons, spies, and terrorists.

Assuming that the building does re-open to the public on schedule, you'll get to see all that and more, as the one-hour tour takes you through various exhibits covering the FBI Academy, the history of gangsters and organized crime, the near-legendary Ten Most Wanted Fugitives program, and the Bureau's newest targets, domestic terrorism and espionage.

What To Do

All thrilling stuff, especially the glass cases full of seized "trophies" from some of America's most infamous crooks, but the biggest hit with the kids these days is the third floor gallery overlooking the FBI's high-tech forensics lab, with its banks of computers, DNA equipment, and scientific instruments capable of finding and identifying an incredible range of clues. And for a bang-up finish, there's a precision firearm skills demonstration with revolvers and automatic weapons (and human-shaped paper targets).

So, where are the X-Files? The Bureau steadfastly denies the existence of any supernatural or paranormal investigative agents, but they wouldn't let me go down to the basement to check, so I guess the truth is still "out there."

Our primary tip for visiting FBI Headquarters is to plan ahead, for all sorts of reasons. The lines can be two hours long and longer, but a call six weeks prior to your trip to your senator or representative's office can sometimes get you on a pre-booked VIP tour, which will whisk you right past the line.

Keep in mind that this is primarily a walking tour. Some allowances can be made for the disabled and strollers, but once again, you'll have to call ahead. And this is a secure facility; that means no pocketknives or pretend-guns, not even your six-year-old's super soaker. No cameras, camcorders or tape recorders either, or cigarettes, food, or drinks for that matter. Think these folks are strict? Hey, they're G-men, right?

The Mall

Across the River

Arlington National Cemetery

**Across Memorial Bridge (about 3/4 mi.)
from Lincoln Memorial
Arlington, VA 22211
(703) 979-4886
www.arlingtoncemetery.org.**

Arlington National Cemetery

Metro: Blue line to Arlington Cemetery

Hours: April-Sept – daily, 8am - 7pm;
Oct-March – daily, 8 am - 5 pm.

Cost: Free.

Adam T. Lass

Among the thousands of men and women buried at Arlington are Washington planner Pierre L'Enfant; President John F. Kennedy, along with First Lady Jacqueline Bouvier Kennedy Onassis and the president's brother, Attorney General Robert F. Kennedy; President and Supreme Court Justice William Howard Taft and Supreme Court Justices Earl Warren, Hugo Black, Oliver Wendell Holmes Jr., Thurgood Marshall, and Potter Stewart; civil rights leader Medgar Evers; journalist and abolitionist Robert Ingersoll; 1950s Hollywood star and much decorated soldier Audie Murphy and actors Constance Bennett and Fay Bainter; 1940s bandleader Glenn Miller, novelists Mary Roberts Rinehart and Dashiell Hammett, boxer Joe Louis; and the Contrabands, 3,800 Civil War fugitive and liberated slaves, their headstones marked with the words "Citizen" or "Civilian." The many memorials include the Iwo Jima Memorial, the Women in Military Service for America Memorial and the Challenger Space Shuttle Memorial.

What To Do

The Pentagon

Arlington, VA 22201
(703) 695-1776
www.defenselink.mil/pubs/pentagon.

The Pentagon

Metro: Yellow or Blue line to Pentagon

Hours: Closed to the public since September 11, 2001.

Cost: Free.

It's the world's largest office building, with three-and-a-half million square feet and 17-plus miles of corridors. It's the nerve center of the mightiest military machine in history. And until September 11th, parts of it were open to the public.

Not any more, of course. As everyone knows, on that date a hijacked plane hit the building, killing 189 people and severely damaging the structure. The Pentagon has been closed to the public ever since.

You can see it from the outside. You can still take a virtual tour on the Pentagon's website. You can read here the facts that you would have found out if you had been able to tour it:

- The Pentagon was conceived as World War II loomed over Europe and America. Ground was broken in the autumn of 1941 – shortly before Pearl Harbor – and the building was opened in January 1943. It was created as such a consciously efficient structure that it was possible, at least for a soldier in good condition, to get from any point in the massive structure to any other point in seven minutes.

- It is the headquarters of the U.S. Department of Defense, employing some 23,000 civilians and military personnel.

- It serves 4,500 cups of coffee and processes 200,000 telephone calls a day (and a million-plus pieces of mail a week).

The Department of Defense is restoring the damaged parts of the Pentagon under a project called "Phoenix," after the mythical bird that rose out of its own ashes. The target date for full restoration is September 11, 2002.

Museum City

Museum City:
The Museums and Galleries

Beyond the great museums at the Mall, Washington probably has the highest ratio of museums to residents of any city in the nation. From doll houses and birds to postage stamps, textiles, news, and women in the arts, there are collections here – including, of course, the rest of the Smithsonian museums – to suit every possible taste, including your whole family's. Here's a probably too incomplete sampling of things to see in between your other activities.

Anacostia Museum and Center for African American History and Culture

1901 Fort Place SE
Washington, DC 20020
(202) 287-2060 (recorded info.); (202) 287-3306
www.si.edu/anacostia

Anacostia Museum and Center for African American History and Culture

Metro: Green line to Anacostia

Hours: Daily 10 am - 5 pm; Closed Dec 25.

Cost: Free.

The Smithsonian's exploration of "American history, society, and creative expression" from an African-American perspective, the Anacostia Museum's ever-changing exhibits cover a wide range. They've included objects and documents from the civil rights movement, sculpture by African-American artists, and photographs of the epic boxing match between Mohammed Ali and George Foreman; you'll want to call ahead or check their website to see what's offered during your visit. (The website also has its own, separate exhibits; recent ones have covered African-American communities of faith, black photographers from 1840 to today, and African-Americans working in the food trades.) The neighborhood within which the museum is located (see "East of the River" in Chapter Three) is rich in African-American history as well.

What To Do

National Geographic Society Explorers Hall

1145 17th Street NW
Washington , DC 20036
(202) 857-7588
www.nationalgeographic.com/explorer

You've read the magazine, you've seen the TV shows – now see National Geographic come to life, as it were. Mostly interactive exhibits cover the natural and human worlds, not unlike a museum of natural history, but a little slicker and a lot smaller. Recent exhibits explored the world of Islam and traced a conservationist's 2,000-mile walk across Africa.

> **National Geographic Society Explorers Hall**
>
> Metro: Red line to Farragut North; Blue, Orange lines to Farragut West
>
> Hours: Mon-Sat, 9 am - 5 pm; Sun 10 am - 5 pm; Closed Dec 25.
>
> Cost: Free.

National Museum of Women in the Arts

1250 New York Avenue NW
Washington, DC 20005
(202) 783-5000
www.nmwa.org

The world's only museum exclusively featuring art by women, the National Museum of Women in the Arts is, not surprisingly, a relative newcomer among DC's galaxy of museums. It opened in 1981, and only came to its present location, a former Masonic temple, in 1987. But with women artists still underrepresented in major museums, this one is worth a visit with children of either gender as a salutary reminder that women have made their marks in the arts in every era (although the museum's collections only begin with the Renaissance). It contains works by the usual subjects – women who have been admitted into the artistic pantheon, like Mary Cassatt, Rosa Bonheur, and Georgia O'Keeffe – along with those by women you never had heard about until now.

> **National Museum of Women in the Arts**
>
> Metro: Red, Blue, Orange lines to Metro Center
>
> Hours: Mon-Sat, 10 am - 5 pm; Sun, noon - 5 pm; Closed New Year's, Thanksgiving, Dec 25.
>
> Cost: Suggested donation – General, $3; Students and senior citizens, $2.

Museum City

National Portrait Gallery

Old Patent Office Building
Eighth and F Streets NW
Washington, DC 20001
(202) 357-1300
www.npg.si.edu.

National Portrait Gallery

Metro: Green, Yellow, Red lines
to Gallery Place/Chinatown

Hours: Closed for renovation
until 2004.

What did First Lady Dolly Madison look like? Or Buffalo Bill? Or writer Gertrude Stein, or Girl Scouts founder Juliette Low, or abolitionist Frederick Douglass?

Washingtonians and visitors alike have found the answers to those questions for years at the Smithsonian's National Portrait Gallery, but, alas, as of this writing, it's closed for renovation. Meanwhile, some of its collections, including its extensive group of portraits of George Washington, are traveling the nation, so watch for them in your town.

National Postal Museum

2 Massachusetts Avenue NE
Washington, DC 20002
(202) 633-9260
www.si.edu/postal

National Postal Museum

Metro: Red line to Union Station

Hours: Daily 10 am - 5:30 pm;
Closed Dec 25.

Cost : Free.

Stamps, stamps, stamps – and, for good measure, letter boxes, Post Office vehicles, postage meters, and anything else that tells the "story of postal history in America" – are on view here in 23,000 square feet of exhibit space under Washington's old Main Post Office, near Union Station. The National Postal Museum is more than an esoteric haunt for mad philatelists – it offers views of American life through the centuries as seen through the lens of what was, until the telephone and then the Internet revolutions, a daily event for millions of Americans.

The Smithsonian maintained a philatelic collection for most of the 20th century, but didn't move it here until 1993. You can see a rare set of misprinted stamps from 1869, a pane of ten-cent Confederate stamps, a postcard salvaged from the wreck of the German zeppelin *Hindenburg*, or the first piece of mail ever flown across the Atlantic; you can find out when the first U.S. postage stamp was issued, or what bird has appeared most often on U.S. stamps.

What To Do

Rock Creek Park Planetarium

Rock Creek Nature Center
5200 Glover Road NW
Washington DC 20015
(202) 426-6829
www.nps.gov/rocr/planetarium

Even in an age of virtual everything, watching the stars come out overhead in a planetarium is thrilling. The only planetarium in the National Park system, this one has specifically educational aims – but the kids probably won't notice that they're being educated. The programs for younger children show them the major constellations; the ones for older kids show the heavens as they'll appear that same night. The Planetarium can provide an indoor-sitting break in a day spent outdoors enjoying Rock Creek Park (see "The Great Outdoors," p. 90).

Rock Creek Park Planetarium

Metro: Red line to Friendship Heights, take E2 bus line toward Ft Totten to Glover and Military Rds, or Red or Green line to Ft Totten, take E2 bus toward Friendship Heights to Glover and Military Rds.

Hours: Sky shows – Sat-Sun, 1 pm for children 4 and older (under-8-year-olds must be accompanied by an adult); 4 pm for children 7 and older; After School program – Wed, 4 pm.

Cost: Free.

Smithsonian American Art Museum

Old Patent Office Building
Eighth and F Streets NW
Washington, DC 20001
(202) 633-8998
www.nmaa-ryder.si.edu

Smithsonian American Art Museum-Renwick Gallery

Pennsylvania Avenue at 17th Street NW
Washington, DC 20006
(202) 357-2700
http://nmaa-ryder.si.edu/collections/renwick

The Renwick is the Smithsonian's museum of American crafts, showing glass, wooden, fabric and other objects from the 19th, 20th, and 21st centuries in an historic mansion across the street from the White House.

At this writing, the Renwick's Grand Salon is also showing 170 paintings and sculpture from the Smithsonian American Art Museum during the latter's renovation.

Smithsonian American Art Museum

Metro: Orange, Blue lines to Gallery Place/Chinatown

Hours: Closed for renovation through 2002, but see Smithsonian American Art Museum-Renwick Gallery, below.

Cost: Free

Smithsonian American Art Museum-Renwick Gallery

Metro: Red line to Farragut North; Blue and Orange lines to Farragut West

Hours: Daily 10 am - 5:30 pm; Closed Dec 25.

Cost: Free.

Museum City

Textile Museum

2320 S Street NW
Washington, DC 20008
(202) 667-0441
www.textilemuseum.org

Textile Museum

Metro: Red line to Dupont Circle

Hours: Mon-Sat, 10 am - 5 pm;
Sun, 1- 5 pm.

Cost: Suggested donation, $5.

What are the clothes you wear actually made of? Find out at the Textile Museum, where, amid the monuments and the history, there's a museum featuring the fabrics of everyday life – literally.

Courtesy Textile Museum

Textile Museum Activity Center

Founded in 1925, Washington's Textile Museum has hands-on interactive exhibits including an Activity Gallery where kids can learn what clothes from around the world are made of. Weekend workshops give young museum-goers a chance to actually create fabrics. (A plus for parents: the Textile Museum is in the heart of Washington's fascinating Dupont Circle neighborhood.)

Washington Dolls' House and Toy Museum

5236 44th Street NW
Washington, DC 20015
(202) 244-0024

Washington Dolls' House and Toy Museum

Metro: Red line to Friendship Heights

Hours: Tues-Sat, 10 am - 5 pm;
Sun, noon - 5 pm.

Cost: General, $4; Seniors, $3;
Children, $2.

Look-but-don't-touch toy museums are always tricky for children, and you have to decide based on your own knowledge of your kids whether this small museum devoted to playthings of the past will be fun or tormenting for them. Most of the items in the collection are from the 19th century, and some are for sale in the museum's gift shop (always a mixed blessing for parents).

What To Do

Other Museums

Alexandria Black History Resource Center

638 N Alfred Street (at Wythe St)
Alexandria, VA 22314
(703) 838-4356
http://ci.alexandria.va.us/oha/bhrc

Once the first public library for Alexandria's black community, this center now houses documents and photos relating to the city's black community.

Alexandria Black History Resource Center

Metro: Yellow or Blue line to Braddock Rd.

Hours: Tues-Sat, 10 am - 4 pm; Sun, 1-5 pm.

Cost: Free.

Art Museum of the Americas

201 18th Street NW
Washington, DC 20006
(202) 458-6016
www.oas.org/museum

The art museum of the Organization of American States exhibits 20th-century works by Latin-American artists.

Art Museum of the Americas

Metro: Orange, Blue lines to Farragut West

Hours: Tues-Sun, 10 am - 5 pm.

Cost: Free.

Athenaeum

201 Prince Street
Alexandria, VA 22314
(703) 548-0035

Athenaeum

Hours: Wed-Sat & Sun 10am - 4 pm.

Cost: Voluntary donation

This exquisite 1852 Classic Revival building was originally a bank, then a church; now it houses an art gallery featuring works by contemporary regional artists. Unless your kids are crazy for art, stop by for the architecture and make a note to yourself for later: the museum closes mid-November through mid-January while the Athenaeum's ballet troupe practices for their popular Holiday performances of *The Nutcracker*. Tickets sell out early due to limited space.

Museum City

B'nai B'rith Klutznick National Jewish Museum

1640 Rhode Island Avenue NW
Washington, DC 20036
(202) 857-6583

B'nai B'rith Klutznick National Jewish Museum

Metro: Red line to Dupont Circle or Farragut; North, or Blue, Orange lines to Farragut West

Hours: Sun-Fri, 10 am - 5 pm; Closed federal holidays.

Cost: Free.

Exhibits on Jewish history, arts, and culture from one of the country's largest collections of Judaica.

Corcoran Gallery of Art

500 17th Street NW
Washington, DC 20006
(202) 639-1700
www.corcoran.org

Corcoran Gallery of Art

Metro: Orange, Blue lines to Farragut West; Red line to Farragut North

Hours: Wed, Fri-Mon, 10 am - 5 pm; Thurs, 10 am - 9 pm.

Cost: Suggested donations; General, $3; Families $5. Free guided tours, 12:30 pm.

The largest art museum in Washington that isn't part of the Smithsonian or government-run, the Corcoran was originally founded as a museum of American art but now houses extensive collections of European art as well.

DAR Museum

1776 D Street NW
Washington, DC 20006
(202) 879-3239
www.dar.org

DAR Museum

Metro: Orange and Blue lines to Farragut West; Red line to Farragut North

Hours: M-F, 8:30 am - 4 pm; Sun, 1-5 pm.

Cost: Free.

What you'd expect at the museum of the Daughters of the American Revolution – Americana: 33,000 pieces of tableware, textiles, furniture, etc., from the Colonial and Federal periods.

What To Do

DEA Museum

700 Army Navy Drive
Arlington, VA 22202
(202) 307-3463
www.usdoj.gov/dea/deamuseum

Washington really does have museums of just about everything – this is the drug enforcement museum from the U.S. Drug Enforcement Administration. If you want to scare your teens and pre-teens away from drugs, this is the place to do it.

DEA Museum

Metro: Blue, Yellow lines to Pentagon

Hours: Open by appointment only Tues-Fri, 10 am - 4 pm.

Cost: Free.

Hillwood Museum and Gardens

4155 Linnean Avenue NW
Washington, DC 20008
(202) 686-8500; toll-free (877) HILLWOOD
www.hillwoodmuseum.org

Fabergé eggs and Native American crafts and 25 acres of beautifully landscaped gardens – the former home of cereal heiress Marjorie Merriweather Post now houses her very eclectic collection of *objets d'art*.

Hillwood Museum and Gardens

Metro: Red line to Van Ness/UDC (but it's a long walk from the Metro station)

Hours: Open by reservation for guided tours only, Tues-Sat, 9 am - 5 pm; Closed Feb and national holidays.

Cost: General, $10; Senior citizens, $8; Students and children under 18, $5.

Kreeger Museum

2401 Foxhall Road NW
Washington, DC 20007
(202) 337-3050
www.kreegermuseum.com

One of Washington's newest art museums, the Kreeger opened in 1994 to exhibit the immense modern and contemporary collection of David and Carmen Kreeger – from Monet, Picasso, and Renoir to Alexander Calder. The building was designed by preeminent contemporary architect Philip Johnson.

Kreeger Museum

Metro: Red line to Tenleytown (but the museum is a one-mile walk from Metro station).

Hours: Tues-Fri for guided tours only (reservations required), 10:30 am and 1:30 pm; Sat tour 10:30 am; open to the general public Sat, 1-4 pm.

Cost: Suggested donation, $5. *Children under 12 not admitted to museum.*

Museum City

Lillian and Albert Small Jewish Museum

701 3rd Street NW
Washington, DC 20001
(202) 789-0900

Lillian and Albert Small Jewish Museum

Metro: Red line to Judiciary Square

Hours: Sun-Thurs, 10 am - 4 pm. Guided tours by appointment.

Cost: Suggested donation, $2.

Housed in Washington's oldest extant synagogue, the Small museum exhibits documents, photographs, and other objects relating to DC's Jewish history.

Lyceum

201 S Washington Street
Alexandria, VA 22314
(703) 838-4994
http://ci.alexandria.va.us/oha/lyceum

Lyceum

Metro: Yellow, Blue lines to King St., bus to King and Washington

Hours: Mon-Sat, 10 am - 5 pm; Sun, noon - 5 pm; Closed major holidays.

Cost: Free.

Built as a public hall in 1839 for meetings (and "quiet reading"), the Lyceum building has been a hospital, a home, and, in 1976, a bicentennial center. It now houses Alexandria's history museum.

National Building Museum

401 F Street NW
Washington, DC 20001
(202) 272-2448
www.nbm.org

National Building Museum

Metro: Red line to Judiciary Square

Hours: Mon-Sat, 10 am - 4 pm; Sun, noon - 4 pm; Closed Thanksgiving, Dec 25, New Year's Day. Public tours daily from 12:30 pm.

Cost: Free.

The place to bring budding architects, this is the country's museum of architecture, design, and urban planning. Its Great Hall is considered a marvel of engineering.

What To Do

Octagon Museum

1799 New York Avenue NW
Washington, DC 20006
(202) 638-3221
www.amerarchfoundation.com

Adam T. Lass

Exhibits on Washington's architectural history, housed in a building that's actually a hexagon.

Octagon Museum

Metro: Blue, Orange lines to Farragut West, Farragut North.

Hours: Tues-Sun, 10 am - 4 pm; Closed Thanksgiving, Dec 25, New Year's Day

Cost: General, $3; Students $1.50.

Phillips Collection

1600 21st Street NW
Washington, DC 20009
(202) 387-2151
www.phillipscollection.org

When the Philips opened in 1921, it was the country's first museum of modern art, exhibiting works by Cézanne, Renoir, and other Impressionist masters. The museum also holds fun programs to introduce kids to art.

Phillips Collection

Metro: Red line to Dupont Circle

Hours: Tues-Wed & Fri-Sat, 10 am - 5 pm; Thurs, 10 am - 8:30 pm; Sun, noon - 5 pm.

Cost: Weekends, General $7.50, Seniors and students, $4, Under 18, free. Weekdays, suggested donation same as weekend admission.

Living History

Washington Slept Here: Living History

It's been the nation's capital for more than two centuries, and a lot of history has happened here. Much of it was in corridors of power like the White House, the Capitol, and the Pentagon, but a lot has gone on in private spaces across the city – in people's homes, a theater, a modern apartment-hotel. Described below are some of the most exciting, followed by a listing of some of the others.

Mount Vernon

George Washington Parkway
Mt. Vernon, VA 22121
Mailing address:
PO Box 110
Mount Vernon, VA 22121
(703) 780-2000
www.mountvernon.org

Washington sleeps here. He was, of course, our first president, the "Father of His Country." But he was also a farmer who loved his farm and his home. (He once said he would "rather be at home at Mount Vernon with a friend or two . . . than be attended at the seat of the government by the officers of State and the representatives of every power in Europe.")

Mount Vernon is the 500-acre estate and mansion where George Washington lived, died, and is buried. It's beautiful and grand – Washington spent almost forty years making it that way.

Mount Vernon

Eight miles south of Alexandria on George Washington Parkway.

Hours: April-Aug – daily, 8 am - 5 pm; Sept-Oct – daily, 9 am - 5 pm; Nov-Feb – daily, 9 am - 4 pm.

Cost: General, $9; Seniors (62-plus) with ID, $8.50; Children 6-11, $4.50; 5 and under, free.

When he inherited the estate in 1761 (from his older half-brother's widow), the house was a seven-room farmhouse on a 2,000-acre estate – a fit enough residence for a colonial farmer, but hardly the mansion of a president. When he died in 1799, the house was topped by a cupola and had seventeen rooms and a two-story "piazza" overlooking the Potomac, and the estate consisted of 8,000 acres.

What To Do

Today the estate at Mount Vernon consists of the 500 acres that were the Mansion House Farm; the house has been restored to its 1799 condition and is visited yearly by millions. You can see a plan of the Mansion House Farm drawn up in 1787 and tour the estate and see the stables and coach house, gardener's house, and other buildings as well as the decorative and kitchen gardens. There is a restaurant and a food court; the latter is open daily from 9:30 a.m. to 5:30 p.m.

College Park Aviation Museum

**1985 Cpl. Frank Scott Drive
College Park, MD 20740
(301) 864-6029
www.avialantic.com/collpark**

No, Washington didn't sleep here. Wilbur Wright flew here.

College Park Aviation Museum

Metro: Green line to College Park

Hours: Daily, 10 am - 5 pm; Closed major holidays.

Cost: General, $4; Seniors, $3; Children 2-18, $2.

Adam T. Loss

This is *the* place in the Washington area for airplane buffs of all ages. College Park Airport is the oldest continuously operating airfield in the world. In 1909, Wright instructed the men who would become the nation's first military pilots here, and two years later, he and his brother Orville built a plane here for the Army's first aviation school.

Wilbur Wright still greets visitors to the museum housed in the airfield – an animatronic Wright, that is. As a museum of aviation, College Park is state-of-the-art. You can see airplanes and helicopters from the early part of the century, some of them cut in half so that visitors can get in and play. There are interactive exhibits – including flight simulators – in every gallery of the museum, as well as real air-traffic control radios at which you can listen in on the controllers at other local airports.

Living History

Frederick Douglass National Historic Site-Cedar Hill

1411 W Street SE
Washington, DC 20020
(202) 426-5961
www.nps.gov/frdo

Cedar Hill was the last home of Frederick Douglass, one of the towering figures of 19th-century America. Born a slave in Maryland in 1817 or 1818, he escaped to the North and freedom at the age of twenty.

At twenty-one, he found what he called his "religion" – the crusade for the abolition of slavery. He spent most of the next thirty years fighting for that cause.

As a propagandist – in print or on the podium – he was unrivaled. He was hired by anti-slavery organizations as a traveling lecturer; he published books, including *The Narrative of the Life of Frederick Douglass, an American Slave*; he was editor and publisher of several abolitionist journals, including *The North Star*.

Frederick Douglass National Historic Site-Cedar Hill

Metro: Green line to Anacostia, transfer to B-2 (Mt. Rainer) bus

Hours: Spring-summer, 9 am - 5 pm; Fall-winter, 9 am - 4 pm.

Cost: Tours $3; reservations suggested.

But Douglass needed action as well as words. In the segregated North, he once refused to leave a whites-only coach on a train (and was thrown off the train for the civil disobedience). He traveled around the nation and Europe, preaching abolition and meeting with other anti-slavery activists, including writer Harriet Beecher Stowe and John Brown, the radical white abolitionist who took up arms against slavery and was eventually executed for leading a raid on a U.S. arsenal at Harper's Ferry (see p. 171). Most consistently, however, for all the years between his own emancipation and that of all America's slaves, Douglass participated in the Underground Railroad, helping as many slaves to freedom as he could.

His passion for freedom may have begun with the anguish of slavery, but it didn't end there. Unlike many abolitionist men, Douglass was quick to see the parallels between the enslavement of black people and the disenfranchisement of women. He was a participant in the first convention for women's rights in Seneca Falls, New York, in 1848, and he continued to agitate for women's suffrage for the rest of his life. By the time of the Civil War, Douglass was one of the nation's most prominent abolitionists. During the war, he met with President Lincoln more than once, at first to protest the treatment of black Union soldiers, later to consult with the president about Lincoln's re-election campaign.

What To Do

Douglass was forty-seven and still in his prime when the Civil War brought victory to the struggle he had given much of his life to. Nowhere near ready to retire, he took up the cause of the next step – equal rights for Black Americans – inveighing against lynching and segregation with the same fire with which he had called for abolition.

He had become a public figure. In 1871, he was named to a commission of inquiry into the status of the island of Santo Domingo, and the next year, the Equal Rights Party nominated him for the U.S. Vice Presidency. (Flamboyant suffragist Victoria Woodhull was the party's presidential candidate; Douglass turned down the nomination to work instead for President Grant's re-election.)

For all those years, he had lived in the North, in Rochester, New York. But in 1872, the same year as the Equal Rights nomination, his Rochester home was destroyed by fire, and he moved back to the South. He bought Cedar Hill in 1877. In 1889, when Douglass was seventy, President Benjamin Harrison appointed him Minister and Consul-General to Haiti. He died at Cedar Hill in 1895, on the evening of a day he had spent at a meeting of the National Council of Women.

Cedar Hill is maintained as a National Historic Site by the National Park Service. It is "dedicated to preserving the legacy" of the 19th century's most famous African-American.

Gadsby's Tavern Museum

134 North Royal Street
Alexandria, VA 22314
(703) 838-4242; fax (703) 838-4270
http://ci.alexandria.va.us/oha/gadsby

Gadsby's Tavern Museum

Metro: Yellow or Blue line to King St., 1-1/2 mi. down hill on King St to North Royal.

Hours: Guided tours – April-Sept: Mon-Sat, 10 am - 5 pm; Sun, 1-5 pm. Oct-March: Mon-Sat, 11 am - 4 pm; Sun, 1-4 pm.

Cost: General, $4; Students 11-17, $2; Children under 11, free.

Washington didn't sleep here, either – it would have cost sixpence a night if he had – but he did eat and drink and celebrate two birthdays here. What's more, you can find out *what* he ate and drank, details usually omitted from consideration by museum planners.

Gadsby's Tavern Museum in the historic district of Alexandria is made up of two once-separate buildings: the inn built in 1770 and run by the English John Gadsby between 1798 and 1808, and what was the City Hotel, built in 1792. Many of the

Living History

leaders of the American Revolution came here to mix, mingle, and party, including future presidents John Adams, Thomas Jefferson, and James Madison, and their French ally, the Marquis de Lafayette.

Museum exhibits cover the history of the inn and the hotel, the architecture, arts, and clothing of the Federal Period, and the food that guests and residents ate.

Mary Mcleod Bethune Council House

1318 Vermont Avenue NW
Washington, DC 20005
(202) 673-2402
www.nps.gov/mabe

Mary Mcleod Bethune Council House

Metro: Orange, Blue lines to McPherson Square

Hours: Mon-Sat, 10 am - 4 pm

Cost: Free.

A National Historic Site, the Mary McLeod Bethune Council House was the Washington home and office of educator and activist Mary McLeod Bethune (1975-1955) and is maintained now to preserve and interpret both her own life and legacy and the lives and accomplishments of the African-American sisters for whom she fought.

Bethune was a quieter kind of hero than Frederick Douglass. Fiery speeches and rabble-rousing were not her medium. Yet she stands near him among the giants of African-American history, the only leader of the struggle for the advancement of black *women* of her time.

She was first and foremost an educator. Although ultimately her stature in her own community gained her the ear of four presidents, she might have listed founding the school that became Bethune-Cookman College in Florida as her greatest accomplishment. History might disagree with her and place more prominently to her credit the founding of the National Council of Negro Women, or her appointment by President Franklin Delano Roosevelt as Special Advisor on Minority Affairs.

The Mary McLeod Council House was both Bethune's home and the head-quarters of the National Council of Negro Women. Visitors to the site can see its furnishings, historic photographs of Bethune and her associates, and the National Archives for Black Women's History.

What To Do

Sewall-Belmont House

144 Constitution Avenue NE
Washington, DC 20002
(202) 546-3989
www.nps.gov/sebe

Sewall-Belmont House

Metro: Red line to Union Station

Hours: Tues-Fri, 11 am - 3 pm; Sat, noon - 4 pm.

Cost: Suggested donation, $3.

A national historic landmark, this 1800 building is one of the oldest houses on Capitol Hill. It was also the home of suffragist Alice Paul and remains the headquarters of the party she founded, the National Women's Party, which worked for women's suffrage and today works for equality for all people. On exhibit here are desks and chairs that belonged to early feminists Susan B. Anthony and Elizabeth Cady Stanton.

Watergate

2600 Virginia Avenue NW
Washington, DC 20037
(202) 965-3000

Watergate

Metro: Orange, Blue lines to Foggy Bottom

Cost: Free to visit; rooms $175-$350 per night and up.

Any pre-teen or teenager with an interest in history and an affection for conspiracy theory will want to see where the events took place that forced the only resignation from the Presidency in American history. It was here – on the sixth floor – on June 17, 1972, that a party of "burglars" broke into the headquarters of the Democratic National Committee to steal documents that might help President Richard M. Nixon's re-election campaign.

Instead, of course, the discovery led to his resignation two years later. The Watergate is still here, but the Democratic National Committee has long since moved to more congenial – and presumably more secure – headquarters.

Adam T. Lass

The Watergate

Living History

Lincoln Died Here

Ford's Theatre-Lincoln Museum

511 10th Street NW
Washington, DC 20004
(202) 347-4833; toll-free, (800) 899-2367
www.fordstheatre.org

Ford's Theatre-Lincoln Museum

Metro: Red, Blue, Orange lines to Metro Center

Closed for renovations through Fall 2002. (See also Theaters, page 107.)

Petersen House

516 10th Street NW
Washington, DC 20004
(202) 426-6830
www.nps.gov/foth/hwld

Petersen House

Metro: Red, Blue, Orange lines to Metro Center

Hours: Daily, 9 am - 5 pm; Closed Dec 25.

Cost: Free.

Surratt House Museum

9118 Brandywine Rd
Clinton, MD 20735
(301) 868-1121 (voice/TTY)
www.surratt.org

Surratt House Museum

Capitol Beltway (I-95) to Exit 7A; right onto Woodyard Rd/Rt 223W; left at second light onto Brandywine Rd.

Hours: Thurs-Fri, 11 am - 3 pm; Sat-Sun, noon - 4 pm; Closed Easter Sunday, July 4, last half of Dec.

Cost: General, $3; Seniors, $2; Children 5-18, $2.

If your children are more than nine or ten, you all know the story. Now you can see where it all happened.

On the night of April 14, 1865 – the Civil War had finally ended five days earlier – President Abraham Lincoln and First Lady Mary Todd Lincoln went to the theater. The play was Tom Taylor's Our American Cousin, a popular comedy of the time; the theater was Ford's Theatre, on Tenth Street, about five or six blocks from the White House.

The play, of course, never reached its conclusion that night. A little after 10 pm, during the third act, Confederate supporter (and actor) John Wilkes Booth entered the president's box and shot him once in the head, leaped to the stage, and – temporarily, as it turned out – made his escape.

What To Do

Fatally wounded but still alive, the president was carried across the street to the nearest house: 453 Tenth Street (now 516 Tenth), then known as the Petersen boarding house. Lincoln lay bleeding all night on the parlor floor of the house. (They had to place him diagonally across the bed – at six feet, five inches, the tall president needed an extra-long bed.) He died at 7:22 the next morning.

Booth, meanwhile, had made his way to the Clinton, Maryland, boardinghouse of the widow Mary Surratt, where he spent the night. On April 26, the most wanted man in the country, Booth was shot to death outside a tobacco shed in Virginia. A few days later, a number of his alleged co-conspirators, including Mrs. Surratt, were arrested. Their trial began on May 9th, and they were hanged on July 7th. It was the first time the U.S. government had executed a woman. More recent research has cast doubt on her participation in the plot.

Ford's Theatre closed immediately after the assassination and the building was used as a warehouse and for other purposes until 1932, when a Lincoln museum was opened there. In 1965-67, it was restored as a theater, reopening in 1968, and now houses both a Lincoln museum and a working theater. (Although at this writing it is under renovation yet again, and is scheduled to re-open in November, 2002.)

All three of those sites – Ford's Theatre, Petersen House, and Surratt House – are now maintained as museums, the first two by the U.S. National Parks Service, the last by the Surratt Society for preservation of the history and culture of mid-19th-century Maryland. Lincoln lovers and budding historians can find them at the sites listed above.

Other Historic Sites

Arlington House – Robert E. Lee Memorial

George Washington Memorial Parkway
Arlington, VA 22201
(703) 557-0613
www.nps.gov/arho

Arlington House-Robert E. Lee Memorial

Metro: Blue line to Arlington National Cemetery

Hours: Daily, 9:30 am - 4:30 pm; Closed Dec 25 and New Year's. Arlington House Grounds and Museum: Oct-March, 8 am - 4:30 pm; April-Sept, 8 am - 6:30 pm.

Cost: Free.

The home of Confederate General Robert E. Lee.

Living History

Clara Barton National Historic Site

5801 Oxford Road
Glen Echo, MD 20812
(301) 492-6245
www.nps.gov/clba

Clara Barton National Historic Site

Hours: Daily guided tours on the hour, 10 am - 4 pm; Closed New Year's, Thanksgiving, Dec 25.

Cost: Free.

Right next door is the Clara Barton National Historic Site, commemorating the life of the founder of the American Red Cross. This house served as her home, as headquarters for the American Red Cross, and as a warehouse for disaster relief supplies. From here, she organized and directed American Red Cross relief efforts for victims of natural disasters and war.

Decatur House Museum

748 Jackson Place NW
Washington, DC 20006
(202) 842-0920
www.decaturhouse.org

Decatur House Museum

Metro: Orange, Blue lines to Farragut West; Red line to Farragut North

Hours: Tues-Fri, 10 am - 3 pm; Sat-Sun, noon - 4 pm.

Cost: General, $4; Student, $2.50.

One of Washington's oldest houses, built in 1818 for Stephen Decatur, naval hero of the War of 1812.

Dumbarton House

2715 Q Street NW
Washington, DC 20007
(202) 337-2288
www.dumbartonhouse.org

Dumbarton House

Metro: Red line to Dupont Circle, then bus D1, D2, or D6.

Hours: Sept-July, Tues-Sat, 10 am - 12:15 pm; Closed federal holidays and Dec 23-Jan 2.

Cost: Donation requested.

This stately house on a hill in Georgetown exhibits furniture and decorative arts of the Federal period.

What To Do

Dumbarton Oaks Museum

1703 32nd Street NW (Georgetown)
Washington, DC 20007
(202) 339-6401
www.doaks.org

A 10-acre garden surrounds this museum of Byzantine and pre-Columbian South American art.

Dumbarton Oaks Museum

Metro: Red line to Dupont Circle, then walk to Georgetown.

Museum hours: Tues-Sun, 2-5 pm; Closed national holidays.

Cost: Free (donations accepted).

Garden hours: March 15-Oct, 2-6 pm; Nov-March, 2-5 pm; Closed during inclement weather, national holidays, Dec 24.

Cost: March 15-Oct: General, $5; Seniors and children, $3; Nov 14-March, free.

Fort Ward Museum and Historic Site

4301 West Braddock Road
Alexandria, VA 22314
(703) 838-4848
http://oha.ci.alexandria.va.us/fortward/

One of the forts that protected the capital during the Civil War.

Fort Ward Museum and Historic Site

Metro: Yellow, Blue lines to King St. (museum is a one-mile walk from Metro station)

Hours: Tues-Sat, 9 am - 5 pm; Sun, noon - 5 pm; Closed Thanksgiving, Dec 25, New Year's.

Cost: Free.

Heurich House Museum and Historical Society of Washington, D.C.

1307 New Hampshire Avenue NW
Washington, DC 20036
(202) 785-2068
www.hswdc.org

A 31-room mansion housing an extensive collection of objects and documents about the city's history, the museum also has a lovely garden.

Heurich House Museum and Historical Society of Washington, D.C.

Metro: Red line to Dupont Circle

Hours: Mon-Sat, 10 am - 4 pm; Closed Memorial Day, July 4, Labor Day week, Dec 24-25, New Year's Eve and Day.

Cost: General, $3; Seniors, students, children, $1.50.

Peirce Mill

Tilden Street and Beach Drive in Rock Creek Park
Washington, DC 20008
(202) 426-6908
www.nps.gov/pimi

See corn ground into flour by hand at this perfectly preserved gristmill from the 1820s. And that's really how 'Peirce' is spelled, at least at the Peirce Mill.

Peirce Mill

Metro: Red line to Cleveland Park

Hours: Wed-Sun, noon - 4 pm; Closed July 4, Thanksgiving, Dec 25, New Year's.

Cost: Free.

Living History

Society of the Cincinnati at Anderson House

2118 Massachusetts Avenue NW
Washington, DC 20008
(202) 785-2040
www.dkmuseums.com/cincin

Society of the Cincinnati at Anderson House

Metro: Red line to Dupont Circle

Hours: Tues-Sat, 1-4 pm.

Cost: Free.

A sort of post-Revolutionary American Legion, the Society of the Cincinnati was founded in 1783 as a patriotic organization by officers of the American army. The museum exhibits Revolutionary War objects and documents.

Stabler-Leadbeater Apothecary Shop Museum

105 S Fairfax Street
Alexandria, VA 22314
(703) 836-3713
www.apothecary.org

Stabler-Leadbeater Apothecary Shop Museum

Metro: Orange, Blue lines to King St.

Hours: Mon-Sat, 10 am - 4 pm;
Sun, 1-5 pm.

Cost: General, $2.50; Students, $2;
Children under 11, free.

George Washington filled his prescriptions here! Unique even in this history-laden town, the Stabler-Leadbeater drugstore operated from 1792-1933. Now it's a museum offering a rare view of how previous centuries dealt with illness.

Woodrow Wilson House Museum

2340 S Street NW
Washington, DC 20008
(202) 387-4062
www.nthp.org/main/sites/wilsonhouse

Woodrow Wilson House Museum

Metro: Red line to Dupont Circle

Hours: Tues-Sun, 10 am - 4 pm.

Cost: General, $5; Students, $2.50.

President Woodrow Wilson lived here after he left the White House, and, amazingly, this is the only presidential museum actually within the boundaries of the city.

What To Do

The Great Outdoors

History is a good thing, and Washington certainly has a lot of it. All indoors. There will come a point while visiting this town when you and your family will start to feel like some new species of cave bat.

Well, you're in for a pleasant surprise. For all of its "halls of history" reputation, the secret we Washingtonians keep to ourselves is that this is actually one of the best outdoor towns, with more park space per capita than any other city in the country.

We're talking massive green spaces here, parks that extend for miles in every direction. Some follow the rivers' and creeks' banks, complete with opportunities for hiking, biking, and canoeing; some are stately promenades between statelier halls of governments; and some are stolen bits of greenery in the middle of urban settings, replete with horn-playing buskers and chessboards. Almost all of them are beautiful – though perhaps none can compete with the Tidal Basin in the middle of the cherry blossom season – and many have as much historical interest as some of the indoor sites you'll be visiting.

And once you get outside the city limits – although not as far outside as you might think – there are actually wild places, including at least one virtually pristine wilderness within a short drive of the heart of Washington.

Inside the City – The Parks

Anacostia Park

Western End of Nannie Helen Burroughs Avenue NE
Washington, DC 20019
www.nps.gov/anac
(202) 426-6905

> **Anacostia Park**
> Metro: Orange line to Deanwood

Along with Rock Creek Park, Anacostia Park is one of Washington's largest and most important outdoor recreation areas. Its 1,200 acres contain an 18-hole golf course and a golf driving range and the exquisite Kenilworth Aquatic Gardens; at its edge are not one, but three marinas and four boat clubs. There are ball fields and dozens of recreation areas, and its untamed parts teem with wildlife, including blue herons and – though not easy to spot – bald eagles.

Great Outdoors

C&O Canal National Park

Georgetown Visitors' Center
1057 Thomas Jefferson Street NW
Washington, DC 20007
(202) 653-5190
Mailing Address: C&O Canal National Historical Park Headquarters
Box 4, Sharpsburg, MD 21782
(301) 739-4200
www.nps.gov/choh

C&O Canal National Park

Georgetown west to Great Falls, MD (13 mi.), then another 171.5 miles to Cumberland, MD.

C&O Canal

A green highway into America's history, the C&O Canal begins as a secret urban oasis, the shade of its ancient oaks and maples, gently rippling waters, and cobblestone walks a cool and inviting break just a few steps away from the hustle and bustle of Georgetown. But strollers quickly discover that it's much more – an endless green highway that winds its way deep into the American Heartland.

The park begins at the intersection of Rock Creek Park and Pennsylvania Avenue (right around the corner from the Kennedy Center) and runs 184.5 miles north to Cumberland, MD. On the way, it passes by an incredible array of gorgeous natural and historic features including Glen Echo Park, Great Falls, Violet's Lock and Seneca State Park, White's Ferry, and Harper's Ferry.

Looking for someplace for the kids to stretch their legs and vocal cords? Alongside the canal's cool waters runs one of the country's longest continuous hiking and biking trails. My daughters were always particularly delighted by the mule-drawn canal boat rides, hosted by canal men and women in period costumes, and the numerous working hand-operated canal locks.

In addition to the canal boats, long stretches of the canal are open to canoeing, and there are several rental centers along its length, including one in Georgetown. Six visitors' centers along the canal offer historical demonstrations, cultural information, and insights into the park's wildlife and natural surroundings.

What To Do

Created late in the eighteenth century, the canal – with its 185 miles of waterway and towpath and its hand-operated wooden locks – was created as part of an extensive network of waterways intended to link the growing country's new industrial centers and access the vast natural resources of the interior.

However, the arrival of steam powered railroads rendered the canal obsolete before it was even complete. Before long, the trains of the B&O Railroad were carrying the loads of coal from Brunswick down through the mountains to Washington, potentially dooming the waterway.

By the 1950s, the canal and its towpath were being used by a handful of woodsmen and hikers, and plans were brewing to pave the whole thing over and turn it into a superhighway. It was saved from that grisly fate by Supreme Court Justice (and avid outdoorsman) William O. Douglas.

Aghast at the thought of losing such a treasure of historical, cultural, geological, and botanical significance, he challenged the opinion-makers of his day to walk the length of the canal with him and then decide for themselves if it should be destroyed. Fifty-eight conservationists joined him in the crusade that 17 years later saw the creation of the C&O Canal National Historic Park.

The canal's construction may date back to the 1800s, but like so much of Washington, DC, the canal was originally conceived by George Washington himself – in this case, as a means of carrying material and passengers past the blockages of the untamed Potomac river. In fact, a remnant of the pilot project he surveyed and supervised can still be seen today.

Designed to bypass a particularly rough section of the river known as the Seneca Breaks, the "Powtowmack Canal" is a favorite of local canoeists and kayakers, my older daughter, Nicole and myself among them. Over the years, I have walked, biked, canoed, and camped along about half of the canal, and I can personally attest to the impression its astonishing beauty can leave on kids and grownups alike.

Great Outdoors

Great Falls Overlook

One quick caveat: this is a historical park. The towpath wasn't paved in the 1800s, and it's still not today, so it can be a little muddy on wet days. This can also make things a little rough on folks in wheelchairs, despite the park's claims of accessibility to the disabled. Also, there are no guardrails between the towpath and the canal. More than one rambunctious child has gotten wet there, but the water is actually quite shallow, and none have been injured to my knowledge.

Only the larger parks and visitors' centers have restrooms and water fountains, and some have shortened seasonal hours. You would be wise to call ahead if you're counting on using them in the off season; you can get more information at the park's Georgetown Visitors' Center. You used to be able to toss a sleeping bag down virtually anywhere along the canal. But in these more civilized times, camping is restricted to 34 camp sites in select areas (there are also two youth hostels), which are generally quite pleasant, with all sorts of amenities that weren't available when Douglas and his chums trekked the canal.

Kenilworth Aquatic Gardens

Inside Anacostia Park
Anacostia Avenue and Douglas Street NE
Washington, DC 20019
(202) 426-6905

Kenilworth Aquatic Gardens

Metro: Orange line to Deanwood

Hours: Daily, 7 am - 4 pm; visitors' center open daily Sept-April, 8 am - 4 pm.

Cost: Free. Guided tours available.

There's something about water lilies and lotuses that strikes a chord in most adults and many children – these are flowers *growing in the water*! Even in a town as full of blossoms as Washington is for much of the year, the 12-acre Kenilworth Aquatic Garden is a special place, not to mention the animals attracted to the wetland: frogs and turtles, of course, but also muskrats and dozens of species of birds. This serene space is close enough to the Capitol to be a ten- or fifteen-minute break from government buildings and monuments, and a lovely spot for a picnic if you're tired of restaurant (or fast-food) lunches.

What To Do

National Zoological Park

3001 Connecticut Avenue NW
Washington, DC 20008
(202) 357-2700
www.si.edu/natzoo

National Zoological Park

Metro: Red line to Woodley Park-Zoo

Hours: Daily, weather permitting:
May 1-Sept 15, grounds 6 am - 8 pm;
buildings, 10 am - 6 pm; Sept 16-April 30,
grounds 6 am - 6 pm; buildings,
10 am - 4:30 pm; Closed Dec 25.

Cost: Free

Hand over hand the great orangutan swings – fifty feet above the ground and *right over your head!* She's "commuting" on the O Line, the system of poles and cables that allows the orangs to travel *uncaged* between the zoo's Ape House and the Think Tank, where humans work with the apes in investigating the nature of thought and learning. (Platforms on the poles prevent the apes from descending until they get to their destinations.)

At the Zoo

The O Line is just one of the thrilling sights at the National Zoo, one of Washington's gems and a must for visiting families. The authors of this book have taken kids and grandkids here for decades, and we never tire of it. (We think they don't either.) It's among the country's grandest zoos, in its size (163 acres), in the variety and number of its inhabitants (more than 5,800 of them, ranging from elephants to hissing cockroaches), in its dedication to presenting them in environments as natural as possible (as in the O Line), and in its beauty (its original design was yet another work of the firm of the great and prolific landscaper Frederick Law Olmsted).

Established by an act of Congress in 1889, the zoo became part of the Smithsonian a year later – and got its first residents, two Indian elephants, a year after that. That was when zoo animals still lived in cages, of course. Now the zoo is a "Bio Park," and the animals are happier – much happier (and current Director Lucy Spelman plans to renovate some of the remaining older sections). Many of the resident species are endangered in the wild; those and many others are part of research projects that, it is hoped, will tell us what we need to know to better protect the environment we share with them.

Great Outdoors

Current exhibits (get a map when you come in) include:

- **The American Prairie:** The fauna and flora of the Great Plains – bison and prairie dogs, surrounded by prairie grasses and wildflowers.

- **Amazonia Exhibit and Science Gallery:** Piranhas, macaws, two-toes sloths and dart-poison frogs live in the under- and above-water environment, while the Science Gallery next door exhibits current research studies on the Amazon bio-system.

- **The Bears:** Long-time favorites at zoos around the world, residents here include Kodiak, brown, spectacled, and sloth bears.

- **Beaver Valley:** North American wildlife – seals and sea lions, otters and hawks, and endangered Mexican wolves.

- **The Bird House:** Toucans, flamingoes, cranes, and pelicans live here – and, New Zealand's national bird, the kiwi (but the kiwi can be seen only on Mondays, Wednesdays, and Fridays).

- **The Cheetah Conservation Station:** See the fastest land animal on earth – and find out what the zoo is doing to preserve this beautiful, endangered species.

- **Elephant House:** Not just elephants – this part of the zoo houses hippos, giraffes, and rhinoceroses as well. You can watch trainers teach the elephants new skills every morning at 11:30.

- **Forest Carnivores:** The smaller ones – fishing cats and coatis.

- **The Great Ape House:** The noble gorillas in their family groups and the very agile orangs remain favorites of young visitors, as they have been for generations.

- **Great Cats:** It's the lions and tigers, including a baby Sumatran tiger.

- **The Invertebrate Exhibit and Pollinarium:** The first is where you'll find the hissing cockroaches (if you want to), along with spiders, octopuses, sea anemones, and spiny lobsters; the Pollinarium next door is home to hummingbirds, butterflies, and the plants they propagate.

- **Lemur Island:** Ring-tailed and red-fronted lemurs frolic among the trees on their very own island.

- **Reptile Discovery Center:** Snakes and lizards, of course, but also turtles and frogs – and the big ones, crocodiles and Komodo dragons.

- **The Small Mammal House:** From tamarins and foxes to the mysterious armadillo.

- **The Think Tank**, mentioned above, where apes and humans study together.

- **Giant Pandas.**

What To Do

In her childhood, my daughter Nicole's second-favorites were the giant pandas. (She gave her heart to the sea otters when she was two.) Ling Ling and Hsing Hsing were the zoo's star attractions for two decades, having been given to the United States by the People's Republic of China on the occasion of President Richard Nixon's historic visit there in 1972. Ling Ling and Hsing Hsing died in 1992 and 1999, respectively, but they've been replaced. Tian Tian and Mei Xiang arrived in 2000, and the zoo has panda stars again.

Rock Creek Park

(Roughly) north from the National Zoo to Maryland
Mailing address: 3545 Williamsburg Lane NW
Washington, DC 20008
(202) 282-1063
www.nps.gov/rocr

See also Old Stone House, Peirce Mill, and Rock Creek Nature Center and Planetarium.

Rock Creek Park
Metro: many
Hours: Daily, 8 am - dusk.
Cost: Free.

What Central Park is to New York City, Rock Creek Park is to Washington – only bigger. Cutting a 1,745-acre swath through the Northwest quadrant of the city and running from the Potomac past the zoo to the Maryland border and beyond, this park is huge, the biggest urban park in the National Park System. Not surprisingly, you can find pretty near every kind of outdoor activity within its irregular borders, from hiking (some of it rugged), cycling (my own favorite – I've loved the bike trail for years), horseback-riding, picnicking, fishing, and bird-watching to soccer, skating, and roller-blading. There are even indoor activities, at the Nature Center, Peirce Mill, and the Old Stone House. You can't camp in the park, but you can get married here. The parkway within the park is closed to vehicular traffic on Sundays, making it a wonderful promenade of Washingtonians of every stripe and persuasion.

Picnic at Rock Creek Park

Note that because of the park's size, it appears on the "What's Nearby" list of several of the neighborhoods in Chapter Three.

Great Outdoors

Rock Creek Nature Center

5200 Glover Road NW
Washington DC 20015
(202) 426-6828
www.nps.gov/rocr

Rock Creek Nature Center

Metro: Red line to Friendship Heights, take E2 bus line toward Ft Totten to Glover and Military Rds, or Red or Green line to Ft Totten, take E2 bus toward Friendship Heights to Glover and Military Rds.

Fun programs like "Aquatic Ecology" and "Layers of the Forest" teach kids of all ages about the nature and the environment.

Tidal Basin

Off the National Mall
Washington, DC

This is it – this is where the cherry trees bloom.

Actually, they bloom all over the city, but the Tidal Basin is where the largest number of them bloom in one place, creating a display of pink and white blooms that is famous around the world. The cherry blossoms have this in common with diamonds – their renown comes not only from their beauty, but from their rarity. The height of the season – usually in mid-April – is brief, and the blossoms are fragile; a frost or a big storm coming at the wrong moment can so abbreviate the moment they're in full bloom that only a lucky few get to see it. For that reason, we don't advise you to plan your DC visit around the cherry blossoms, but rather to take them as a lucky break should they show their full glory while you're here.

What To Do

Other Parks

Lafayette Square

16th St and Pennsylvania Avenue NW
Washington, DC 20006
(202) 755-7798

The park across the street from the White House.

Meridian Hill Park (Malcolm X Park)

Florida Ave between 15th and 16th Streets
Washington, DC 20009

Separate from, but officially part of, Rock Creek Park. In the 1970s, the City Council renamed Meridian Hill "Malcolm X Park" in honor of the fiery Black Nationalist, who once spoke here. The park contains a beautiful waterfall and a number of interesting statues, including one of Joan of Arc.

U.S. National Arboretum

3501 New York Avenue NE
Washington, DC 20002
(202) 245-2726
www.usna.usda.gov

A 44-acre botanic garden, with aquatic plants, Asian and conifer collections, the National Grove of State Trees, the Friendship Garden, the Native Plant Collections, the National Herb Garden, and 22 columns from the Capitol. It's particularly thrilling in the late spring

> **U.S. National Arboretum**
>
> Metro: (weekends, holidays) Red line to Union Station, transfer to shuttle bus; (weekdays) Blue, Orange lines to Stadium-Armory, transfer to MetroBus B-2 to Bladensburg Road.
>
> Hours: Daily, 8 am - 5 pm; Closed Dec 25.
>
> Cost: Free.

when the azaleas or rhododendrons are in bloom. (Actually, in the late spring, Washington often seems like one immense azalea garden – azalea lovers can find them anywhere and everywhere in the city.)

Great Outdoors

Not Far Away – Waterfalls and Water Slides

Great Falls

In C&O Canal National Historical Park
11710 MacArthur Blvd.
Potomac, MD 20854
(301) 299-9361

Great Falls

Hours: Daily, dawn to dusk.

Cost: $4 per noncommercial vehicle

Great Falls Overlook

Adam T. Lass

Eight miles outside of DC, at the very end of MacArthur Boulevard, the park that surrounds the C&O Canal and the river doubles in width and with good reason. As you park your car in the ample lot, you can already hear a low rumble – or perhaps just feel it in your feet – and feel on your face a feathery bit of moisture in the air. You're in for a real treat.

Just over a small bridge, and past the towpath and the old Great Falls Tavern, is the beginning of a wooden boardwalk that will carry over a series of islands (each its own protected ecosystem, as the plaques will tell you) and on to the edge of Mather Gorge, where you can experience the endless hypnotic thundering of the Potomac's Great Falls. A hundred feet below, you can see (expert) kayakers who have paddled up to the foot of the falls to frolic in the powerful surging surf.

Want to get a little closer? The blazed trail that takes hiker/climbers right down to the edge of the water has been one the great joys of my life both as a youth – it got me started in both free-hand and roped rock climbing – and as a parent, when I taught my older daughter those same skills there and look forward to doing the same with my younger daughter in a few years. But I recommend this for accompanied, responsible kids *only*, as there are a number of drownings each year, and the trail has no railings between it and a deceptively fast moving river.

Be sure to check out the visitors' center at the old inn. The rangers will be only too glad to help you plan your visit with an orientation to the park. There are also exhibits that tell the story of the Patowmack Canal and the park resources.

What To Do

Six Flags America – Maryland

13710 Central Avenue
Largo, MD
(301) 249-1500
www.sixflags.com/parks/america

I must confess that I am a theme park wimp. While I am quite willing to rappel 100 feet down a sheer rock wall or ride a canoe through genuinely dangerous rapids, Ferris wheels make me queasy, and just the thought of the Bat-Wing at Six Flags makes me want to kiss the ground. Still, for millions of American kids, there is no better vacation than one that is spent whirling, twirling, and zooming on the 100-plus rides, shows, and other attractions available at DC's only local theme park. There is an additional charge for rock climbing, the Skycoaster, and Go-Karts (hmmm, now Go-Karts sound like fun). Six Flags sports the area's largest water park, the 25-acre Paradise Island Waterpark, with 13 different ways to get wet, wet, wet. In addition to all the big, twisting water slides and flumes and the pool with waves up to four feet high, there is an activity pool for littler kids and a lazy river (for the sane ones).

Six Flags America - Maryland
Hours: Opening hours vary: 7 days/week in summer; weekends in spring and fall; closed in winter.
Cost: General, $35.99;Seniors, children under 54 inches, and people with disabilities, $23.99; Children under 3, free (extra fees for certain attractions); parking, $9.

Sports

Spectator Sports: Teams and Venues

There are only a few great sport towns . . .

Towns like New York, whose football team has a long, glorious tradition (it was once coached by Vince Lombardi himself) and four Super Bowl trophies on the shelf – oh wait, that's Washington's own Redskins . . . (Not recently you say? Well, the team that won the Super Bowl two years ago was Baltimore's own Ravens, 30 minutes up the road.)

So maybe we should talk about towns like Chicago, where you can watch superhuman players like Michael Jordan sail to the basket – no, Mike is currently cranking out forty-point games for the Washington Wizards.

Okay, how about towns like Pittsburgh, home to a perennial Stanley Cup threat like the Capitals – oops, they play in downtown DC too.

How about the coolest old-style baseball stadium? Hands down, it's Camden Yards, home of the Baltimore Orioles. You want a regular NCAA contender? As I write this, the Maryland Terps are in the Final Four for the second year in a row.

In fact, Washington is an incredibly cool sports town, where on almost any day or night of the year, you can catch something competitive. Add in nearby Baltimore and Annapolis, and you've got one Major League Baseball team, (and a half-dozen hot minor league teams), two NFL teams, hockey, two basketball teams, two soccer teams, Navy Football, and dozens of highly competitive college teams. If you're a family of sports fans, you've come to the right place.

Here are the major teams and sports venues in Washington.

What To Do

Basketball

Washington Wizards

Washington's NBA basketball team, starring Michael Jordan.

MCI Center

601 F Street NW
Washington, DC 20005
(202) 661-5050, ext. 44
www.nba.com/wizards, www.mcicenter.com

The Washington Mystics (Women's Basketball), the Washington Capitals (NHL Hockey), the Washington Power (Professional Lacrosse), and the Georgetown Hoyas (NCAA Basketball) teams also play here.

MCI Center

Metro: Red, Yellow, Green lines to Gallery Pl or Red, Blue, Orange lines to Metro Center.

Tickets $19-$77.

Washington Mystics

MCI Center (see above)
www.washingtonmystics.com

The WNBA women's basketball team.

Washington Mystics

Tickets $8-$37.

Football

Washington Redskins

The local NFL team.

FedEx Field

1600 Raljon Road
Hyattsville, MD 20785
(301) 276-6000
www.redskins.com

FedEx Field

Metro: Blue line to Addison Rd, Orange line to Cheverly or Landover, transfer to shuttle bus.

Officially sold out forever, but $75-$100 through re-sale ads in *Washington Post* classifieds.

Sports

Hockey

Washington Capitals

MCI Center (see above)
www.washingtoncaps.com

The National Hockey League team, now starring Jaromir Jagr.

Washington Capitals
Tickets, (301) 336-CAPS, $19-$60.

Lacrosse

Washington Power

MCI Center (see above)
(301) 324-1755
www.washingtonpower.net

Professional Lacrosse.

Washington Power
Tickets $7.50-$150.

Soccer

DC United

RFK Stadium
2300 E Capitol Street SE
Washington, DC 20003
(703) 478-6600
www.dcunited.com

Major League Soccer (men's).

DC United
Metro: Blue, Orange lines to Stadium Armory
Tickets $12-$35.

Washington Freedom

RFK Stadium (see above)
(202) 5473137
www.washingtonfreedom.org

Watch international star Mia Hamm play with the Washington's women's soccer team.

Washington Freedom
Tickets $12-$22.

What To Do

All Singing, All Dancing – the Performing Arts

Befitting its status in the nation, Washington has more theaters, concert halls, and performance spaces than almost any other city in the country, covering the gamut from the grand to the garage, and from the classics to the most avant-garde.

The jewel in the crown, of course, is the John F. Kennedy Center for the Performing Arts, which by itself includes most of the latter range. But there are rock venues, dance theaters, wildly experimental performance-art spaces, and community theater all over the city and in every suburb.

Below are the city's most significant spaces, followed by a brief listing of other theaters and community theaters around the greater Washington area.

TICKETPLACE

Old Post Office Pavilion
1100 Pennsylvania Avenue NW
Washington, DC 20004
(202) TICKETS

TICKETPLACE is the only same-day discount ticket outlet for Washington area theaters and concert halls. For a family of three or more, it can provide a substantial reduction in the cost of an afternoon or evening watching a play or listening to a concert.

TICKETPLACE

Metro: Orange, Blue lines to Federal Triangle

Hours: Tues-Fri, noon - 6 pm; Sat, 11 am - 5 pm.

Performing Arts

Some of Everything

John F. Kennedy Center for the Performing Arts

2700 F Street NW
Washington, DC 20566
(202) 467-4600; toll-free, (800) 444-1324
www.kennedy-center.org

Kennedy Center/ Photo by Carol Pratt

John F. Kennedy Center for the Performing Arts

From musical celebrations for and performed by children like 2002's "Children of Uganda" to the nation's premiere young people's chamber orchestra, the Kennedy Center offers more performances for children and parents to enjoy together than any other venue in the nation. A national treasure and a must-see for every family visiting Washington, the center entertains audiences numbering in the millions every year with 3,000 performances of musical and theater works – from the country's favorite musicals to opera, symphony, mainstream and experimental theatre, dance, and film, including free performances daily of all or any of the above.

Until 1971, we had no national performance space; until 1958, we didn't even have an official dream of one. It was in that year that President Dwight Eisenhower signed the legislation that would build the center. It took thirteen years to make it a reality; in the intervening time, the assassination of President John F. Kennedy (who had taken an active role in fundraising for the center-to-be) in 1963 demanded a tribute, and what better one than to dedicate the center to him? Pre-eminent American architect Edward Durrell Stone was selected as the architect for the center, and it opened September 8, 1971. Fittingly, its inaugural performance was a Requiem Mass in Kennedy's memory by the nation's pre-eminent composer-conductor Leonard Bernstein.

John F. Kennedy Center
for the Performing Arts

Metro: Orange, Blue lines to Foggy Bottom, transfer to free shuttle.

Hours: Free tours – M-F, 10 am - 5 pm; Sat-Sun, 10 am - 1 pm.

What To Do

It has been added to extensively since then. Forty-one nations have presented gifts to grace its public spaces, including, in the Opera House alone, the African textiles, arts, and crafts that decorate the Box Tier, the fifty-foot chandelier from Austria inside the great dome, and the Matisse "Birds of the Air" and "Fish of the Sea" murals from France at the Box Tier. Today the Center consists of six theaters: the Eisenhower Theater, the Opera House, the Concert Hall, the Terrace Theater, the Theater Lab, and the American Film Institute Theater. Even in the unlikely event that there's nothing playing that suits your family's tastes, the Center is worth a visit as a sight in its own right and as a nation's living tribute to the arts. The view from the Roof Terrace alone provides an unrivalled panorama of Washington and Virginia (including the Jefferson Memorial and the Washington Monument).

Warner Theatre

1299 Pennsylvania Avenue NW
Washington, DC 20004
(202) 628-1818
www.warnertheatre.com

Warner Theatre

Metro: Red, Blue, Orange lines
to Metro Center.

It's only one stage, not almost a dozen, but what a stage! A grandiose restored former vaudeville palace and movie theater from 1924, the Warner now puts on everything from Broadway musicals to stand-up comedy to dance performances and pop music and symphony concerts – and often with the brightest stars in their fields, like pop megastar Prince and comic Paula Poundstone.

Other Music Venues

Carter Barron Amphitheatre

4850 Colorado Avenue NW at 16th St (in Rock Creek Park)
Washington, DC 20011
(202) 426-0486 (concert line)
www.nps.gov/rocr/cbarron

In addition to concerts, the Carter Barron hosts a two-week free Shakespeare festival every summer.

Performing Arts

DAR Constitution Hall

1776 D Street NW
Washington, DC 20006
(202) 628-4780
www.dar.org/conthall

DAR Constitution Hall

Metro: Orange and Blue lines to Farragut West; Red line to Farragut North

Washington's largest concert hall, Constitution Hall made headlines in 1939 by canceling contralto Marian Anderson's scheduled concert when someone found out Anderson was black. The hall has reformed since and hosted a galaxy of famous African-Americans including Mohammed Ali and Duke Ellington; Anderson subsequently appeared there. Most concerts there now are pop music; Bonnie Raitt, for instance, is on a bill as this book goes to press.

Lisner Auditorium at George Washington University

730 21st Street NW
Washington, DC 20052
(202) 994-6800, (202) 994-1500 (24-hr. concert line)
www.gwu.edu/~lisner

Music, dance and theater performed by local and visiting artists.

Lisner Auditorium at George Washington University

Box office open Tues-Fri, 11 am - 5 pm.

Theater

Arena Stage

1101 Sixth Street SW
Washington, DC 20024
(202) 488-3300
www.arena-stage.org

Arena Stage

Metro: Green line to Waterfront-SEU

The capital's much-acclaimed serious theater, the Arena produces works across two millennia of theatre, from the ancient Greeks to today's cutting-edge drama.

Ford's Theatre-Lincoln Museum

511 10th Street NW
Washington, DC 20004
(202) 347-4833, (800) 899-2367
www.fordstheatre.org

Ford's Theatre-Lincoln Museum

Metro: Red, Blue, Orange lines to Metro Center

(See also "Museums")

Closed for renovation through Fall 2002.

What To Do

GALA Hispanic Theater

2437 15th Street NW
Washington, DC 20009
(202) 234-0219 or (202) 234-7174
www.galadc.org

GALA Hispanic Theater

Metro: Green, Yellow, Red lines to Gallery Place/Chinatown

From the high poetic drama of the plays of Spanish playwright Federico Garcia-Lorca to contemporary plays like *Kiss of the Spider Woman*, the Gala has been staging plays from Spain and Latin America in English and Spanish since 1976.

National Theatre

1321 Pennsylvania Avenue NW
Washington, DC 20004
(202) 628-6161
www.nationaltheatre.org

National Theatre

Metro: Red, Blue, Orange lines to Metro Center

One of the oldest theaters in the country (it was built in 1835), and still one of the best, the National calls itself – not without reason – the "theater of presidents." Today it offers Broadway musicals like *Saturday Night Fever* and *The Full Monty*.

Shakespeare Theatre

450 7th Street NW
Washington, DC 20004
(202) 547-1122, toll-free (877) 487-8849, TTY (202) 638-3863
www.shakespearedc.org

Shakespeare Theatre

Metro: Red, Yellow, Blue, Orange lines to Gallery Pl/Chinatown

Formerly housed in the Folger Library, the widely acclaimed company is DC's main venue for classical works by the Greek playwrights, other Elizabethans, and occasionally, modern masters like Lillian Hellman, in addition to its staple Shakespeare productions.

Studio Theatre

1333 P Street NW
Washington, DC 20005
(202) 332-3300
www.studiotheatre.org

Studio Theatre

Metro: Red line to Dupont Circle

One of the District's leading stages for contemporary drama, the Studio produces the work of such playwrights as Tom Stoppard.

Colleges

For the College-Bound: Colleges and Universities

There may or may not be a time for every purpose under heaven, but there's a college in Washington for every possible purpose from peace studies to war, from fine arts to theology. More than a dozen major colleges and universities have their campuses here, including liberal arts schools, colleges of law and medicine, the nation's pre-eminent historically black university, and America's foremost college for the deaf and hearing impaired.

Whether or not you're traveling with a college-bound child – and whether or not your child wants to go to school here – Academia's presence in Washington is almost as influential as the government's; whole neighborhoods serve as giant campuses for one or another of the schools, like Howard University in U Street/Shaw, or Georgetown University in (of course) Georgetown. And the number of students in Washington colors life on the streets (as well as in the pubs and clubs) of the whole city.

If you are thinking of sending a child to college here, the number and variety of schools takes on a more immediate relevance. You may want to visit one or more of the campuses while you're visiting; the next chapter of this book, "The City: A Few Cool Neighborhoods," lists the best-known schools among the highlights of their neighborhoods. High-school age visitors may well want to have at least a quick look at some of them, but even if college is way off in your kids' future, you may want to check out what some of these urban campuses are like.

What To Do

American University

4400 Massachusetts Avenue NW
Washington, DC 20016
(202) 885-1000
www.american.edu

Catholic University of America

620 Michigan Avenue NE
Washington, DC 20064
(202) 319-5000
www.cua.edu

Corcoran College of Art and Design

500 17th Street NW
Washington, DC 20006
(202) 639-1800
www.corcoran.org/college

Gallaudet University

800 Florida Avenue NE
Washington, DC 20002
(202) 651-5000
www.gallaudet.edu

George Mason University

4400 University Drive
Fairfax, VA 22030
(703) 993-1000
www.gmu.edu

George Washington University

2121 Eye Street NW
Washington, D.C. 20052
(202) 994-1000
www.gwu.edu

George Washington University at Mount Vernon College

2100 Foxhall Road NW (in Georgetown)
Washington, DC 20007
(202) 242-6600

Georgetown University

37th and O Streets NW
Washington, DC 20057
(202) 687-0100
www.georgetown.edu

Howard University

2400 Sixth Street NW
Washington, DC 20059
(202) 806-6100
www.howard.edu

National Defense University

Ft. Lesley J. McNair
P Street
Alexandria, VA 22301
(703) 545-6700
www.ndu.edu

Southeastern University

501 I Street SW
Washington, DC 20024
(202) 488-8162
www.seu.edu

Strayer College

2730 Eisenhower Avenue
Alexandria, VA 22314
(703) 329-9100
and
3045 Columbia Pike
Arlington, VA 22204
(703) 329-9100

Trinity College

125 Michigan Avenue NE
Washington, DC 20017
(202) 884-9000
www.trinitydc.edu

University of the District of Columbia

4200 Connecticut Avenue NW
Washington, DC 20008
(202) 274-5000
www.udc.edu

3 The City: A Few Cool Neighborhoods

Washington may be the great repository of our country's history, planned on an orderly grid and shaped by the same grand events that shaped us as a people, but it's also a genuine American city, with vibrant neighborhoods shaped by the residents who have made and continue to make their lives there. And those neighborhoods have blossomed far beyond the wildest dreams of Lafayette and Washington.

As you saw in Chapter One, the city is roughly diamond shaped and is composed of four quarters (Northeast, Northwest, Southeast, and Southwest) around the central hub of the Capitol building. That's the most detail visitors usually hear about. But any local can tell you that it's in the neighborhoods where real life takes place.

In this chapter we'll look at several of the more popular and interesting neighborhoods, covering how to get there (and how to get around once you're there), a little bit of history, and what they offer that is of particular interest to both parents and kids.

You might also want to check out organized tours. Two agencies – one federal, one city – prepare many tours of the city:

Black History National Recreation Trail

National Park Service, National Capitol Region
Office of Public Affairs
1100 Ohio Drive SW
Washington, DC 20242
(202) 619-7222

DC Heritage Tourism Coalition

1250 H Street NW #850
Washington, DC 20005
(202) 661-7581

A Few Cool Neighborhoods

Inside the District

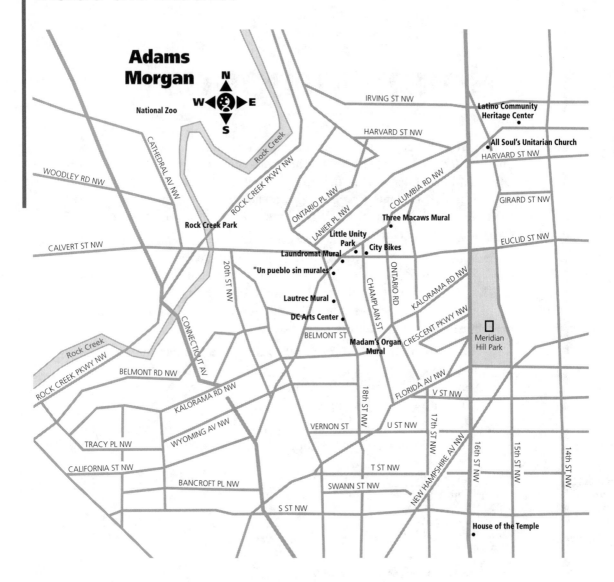

Adams Morgan

National Zoo

N
W E
S

IRVING ST NW

HARVARD ST NW

Latino Community Heritage Center

All Soul's Unitarian Church

HARVARD ST NW

WOODLEY RD NW

CATHEDRAL AV NW

ROCK CREEK PKWY NW

Rock Creek

ONTARIO PL NW

LANIER PL NW

COLUMBIA RD NW

GIRARD ST NW

EUCLID ST NW

Rock Creek Park

Three Macaws Mural

CALVERT ST NW

20th ST NW

Little Unity Park

Laundromat Mural

City Bikes

"Un pueblo sin murales"

CHAMPLAIN ST

ONTARIO RD

KALORAMA RD NW

CRESCENT PKWY NW

Lautrec Mural

DC Arts Center

BELMONT ST

Madam's Organ Mural

Meridian Hill Park

CONNECTICUT AV

Rock Creek

ROCK CREEK PKWY NW

BELMONT RD NW

KALORAMA RD NW

18th ST NW

FLORIDA AV NW

V ST NW

16th ST NW

15th ST NW

14th ST NW

WYOMING AV NW

VERNON ST

U ST NW

17th ST NW

NEW HAMPSHIRE AV NW

TRACY PL NW

CALIFORNIA ST NW

T ST NW

BANCROFT PL NW

SWANN ST NW

S ST NW

House of the Temple

Adams Morgan

Adams Morgan

NW between Conn. Ave, Irving St, 16th St and R St.

Located about two miles north of the White House between 16th Street and Connecticut, the word that best describes Adams Morgan is funk, as in bubbling bopping jazzy coolness. And it wears that funk on its sleeve, so to speak, with a series of brilliantly colored building-side murals that must be seen to be believed.

Adams Morgan

Metro: Red line to Woodley Park/Zoo (unless otherwise specified)

The corner of 18th Street NW and Columbia Road marks the center of a fantastic multicultural bazaar that thumps and buzzes to a heady mix of African and Latino beats. Not surprisingly, this ethnic hot house has spawned an incredible array of restaurants offering everything from fine Italian pesto and those little fried Andean burrito-y things to authentic New Orleans beignets and gumbo and, at my last count, three Ethiopian restaurants with totally different approaches to spicing (my favorite is still the blistering Ber Ber fish at the Red Sea).

Be sure to stop by and see my friends at City Bikes just off 18th Street and Champlain – you can't miss them under the giant bike-riding cows – for rental bikes by the day or the hour. And be sure to get a Cherry Garcia ice cream cone afterwards at Ben and Jerry's.

Also in the Neighborhood
- *National Zoo*
- *Rock Creek Park*

A Few Cool Neighborhoods

What's Nearby

All Soul's Unitarian Church

1500 Harvard Street NW
Washington, DC 20009
(202) 332-5266
www.all-souls.org

One of Washington's oldest congregations, now (in the church's own words), a "historic, theologically plural, multi-cultural congregation committed to social justice." Among its founders in 1821 were future President John Quincy Adams and future Vice President and Secretary of State John C. Calhoun.

City Bikes and "Cows on a Bike Mural"

2501 Champlain Street NW
Washington, DC 20009
(202) 265-1564
www.citybikes.com

The charming "Cows on a Bike" was painted in 1991 by Sarah Lee Terrat and provoked a local controversy when City Bikes was cited for illegal advertising for putting it up. Neighborhood protests supporting the mural forced the city to back down.

District of Columbia Arts Center

2438 18th Street NW
Washington, DC 20009
(202) 462-7833
www.dcartscenter.org

District of Columbia Arts Center

Hours: Wed-Thurs & Sun, 2-7 pm, Fri-Sat, 2-10 pm; theater holds events Wed-Sun nights

Cost: Prices vary with events

A renowned local visual and performing arts space for cutting-edge young artists.

House of the Temple

1733 16th Street NW
Washington, DC 20009
(202) 232-3579
www.dcgrandlodge.org/dcsites.htm

House of the Temple

Hours: Open for tours M-F, 8 am - 2 pm

Cost: Free

A Masonic meeting hall and museum of Masonic history and headquarters for the Scottish Rite of Masonry in the Southeast.

Adams Morgan

Laundromat Mural

1728 Columbia Road
Washington, DC 20009

Painted by local youths in 1998 as a tribute to Adams Morgan's diversity.

Lautrec Mural

2461 18th Street NW
Washington, DC 20009

A portrait of French artist Henri de Toulouse-Lautrec, painted in Lautrec's own style in 1980 by local restaurateur Andre Nevaux.

Little Unity Park

Champlain and 18th Street
Washington, DC 20009

A vest-pocket community park in front of City Bikes, the site of sculptor Jerome Meadows' take on Adams Morgan's diversity, the nearly monumental "Carrying a Rainbow on Your Shoulder."

Lautrec Mural

Latin American Youth Center and Latino Community Heritage Center

1419 Columbia Road
Washington, DC 20009
(202) 319-2225

Exhibits in words and pictures evoke Latino life in the United States in the center sponsored by the Historical Society of Washington, DC, and the Smithsonian Institutions.

Latin American Youth Center and Latino Community Heritage Center

Metro: Green line to Columbia Heights

Open: M-F 9 am - 8 pm;
Sat 9 am - 4 pm

Cost: Free

Madam's Organ Mural

2461 18th Street NW
Washington, DC 20009

A bare-breasted belle painted by Charlie Hababananda advertising the Adams Morgan blues-and-bluegrass club, Madam's Organ.

A Few Cool Neighborhoods

Three Macaws Mural

1706 Columbia Road
Washington, DC 20009

Another tribute to the neighborhood's diversity (the three macaws come from South America, Asia, and Africa), this one by artist G. Byron Peck

"Un pueblo sin murales" ("A city without murals")

1779 Columbia Road
Washington, DC 20009

The oldest and most lavish of the Adams Morgan murals, this one was painted in the 1970s by Chilean artists Carlos Salozar and Felipe Martinez, refugees from the 1973 coup in Chile by General Augusto Pinochet.

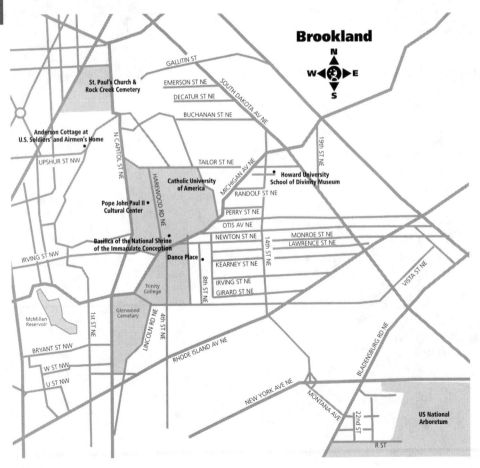

Brookland

Brookland

Straddles North Capital St, the dividing line between NE and NW, between Gallatin and Franklin Sts.

Washington's "Little Rome" has the most amazing selection of grand Christian architecture this side of Constantinople – not surprisingly, since it's home to more than 60 Catholic institutions including Catholic University.

Yeah, I know, this is not hot stuff for any but the most exceptional six-year-old, but older kids may be awed by the splendor of the Basilica of the Shrine of the Immaculate Conception. And any teenager seriously thinking about matters religious, philosophical, or historical will be interested in collections such as the Howard University School of Divinity Museum and the Pope John Paul II Cultural Center.

Brookland

Metro: Red line to Brookland/CUA

With its long history as an integrated neighborhood, Brookland also sports a rich African-American heritage. African-American architects have long had more work in Washington than in many parts of the nation; Brookland contains thirteen International-style houses designed in the 1930s by then-well known architects Hilyard Robinson and Howard H. Mackey. (They built Ralph Bunche house for the Nobel Peace Prize winner). Other famous black Brookland residents have included singer Pearl Bailey, poet Sterling Brown, HUD Secretary Robert Weaver, Senator Edward Brooke, and historian Rayford Logan.

Also in the Neighborhood
• *Catholic University of America*
• *U.S. National Arboretum*

A Few Cool Neighborhoods

What's Nearby

Anderson Cottage at U.S. Soldiers' and Airmen's Home

Rock Creek Church Road and Upshur Street
Washington, DC 20011
(202) 730-3556

Anderson Cottage at U.S. Soldiers' and Airmen's Home

Hours: Tours by appointment only.

Abraham Lincoln wrote the Emancipation Proclamation in this cottage, which lies on the grounds of the U.S. Soldiers' and Airmen's Home (once called the Old Soldiers' Home). Lincoln used the cottage during his presidency as a respite from the pressures of the White House.

Basilica of the National Shrine of the Immaculate Conception

4th Street and Michigan Avenue NE
Washington, DC 20001
(202) 526-8300
www.nationalshrine.com

Basilica of the National Shrine of the Immaculate Conception

Hours: Daily, 7 am - 7 pm.

Cost: Free.

It's definitely awesome. This is the largest Catholic church in the nation. Built in 1920 in an eclectic mix of Byzantine, Romanesque, Renaissance, and contemporary styles, the whole is far greater than the sum of its parts. The Basilica should impress even the children by the sheer grandeur of its massive mosaic-covered dome and the bell tower reaching toward the sky. The mosaics and other art works inside are also impressive.

Dance Place

3225 8th Street NE
Washington, DC 20017
(212) 269-1600
www.danceplace.org

The Dance Place describes itself as Washington's "hub of dance activity." Appropriately, it focuses on African-American dance and dancers, holding an annual two-day festival called "Dance Africa America."

Brookland

Howard University School of Divinity Museum

1400 Shepard Street NE
Washington, DC 20017
(202) 806-0750

Older children and teens, especially those interested in careers in the ministry, will be moved by this treasure house of religious artifacts from all over, including extensive collections of Ethiopian and Byzantine objects.

Howard University School of Divinity Museum

Hours: Tours by appointment only.

Pope John Paul II Cultural Center

3900 Harewood Road NE
Washington, DC
(202) 635-5400
www.jp2cc.org

Pope John Paul II Cultural Center

Hours: Tues-Sat, 10 am - 5 pm; Sun, 12 - 5 pm.

Cost: Voluntary donation.

Creating a virtual stained glass window is just one activity in the interactive galleries here. The research facilities are adult-oriented, but the exhibits on faith and the work of Pope John Paul II are of interest to a wider range of visitors, including teens and even sophisticated pre-teens. The Center is housed in a stunning modern building by architect Leo Daly.

St. Paul's Church-Rock Creek Cemetery

Rock Creek Church Road & Webster Street NW
Washington, DC 20011

The only extant colonial era church in Washington, dating to 1775, St. Paul's is across the street from the Anderson

St. Paul's Church-Rock Creek Cemetery

Hours: Cemetery open daily, 8 am - dusk.

Cost: Free.

Cottage (above). The cemetery next door holds a sculpture by pre-eminent 19th-century American sculptor Augustus St. Gaudens, housed in a mausoleum designed by equally famous architect Stanford White.

A Few Cool Neighborhoods

Capitol Hill

From H Street (NW/NE) to M Street (SW/SE) and
from First Street (NW/SE) to 13th Street (NE/SE).

Capitol Hill

Metro: Red line to Union Station; Blue,
Orange lines to Capitol South, Eastern
Market, Navy Yard

Because the Capitol building itself is at the exact center of all four of Washington's quadrants, Capitol Hill also straddles all quadrants, so expressing addresses can get a little funny around here. Washington planner Pierre L'Enfant believed that the legislature ought to be the central pivot of the new republic's civic life, even (or perhaps especially) more central than the President's residence. So he placed the Congress' permanent home high up on "Jenkin's Hill," where it could literally overlook the capital. Then, to drive the point home, he made it the center point for DC's quadrants and the starting point for all streets and house numbers.

Cap Hill's most prominent feature is, of course, the Capitol building itself, looming over the mall between Constitution and Independence Avenues. But don't underestimate this quaint little neighborhood tucked into the congressional shadow. It's more than just gas-lit, tree-lined streets and exquisite 19th-century row houses (although it is that, too). This part of town has some of the best stuff for kids in Washington, including the Children's Museum, Union Station, and the Folger Shakespeare Library.

In addition to the area's plethora of historic sites, parents will undoubtedly enjoy some of the finest restaurants in the city, and parents and kids alike will get into the funky splendor of the Eastern Market.

Also in the Neighborhood

- Bartholdi Fountain
- Capitol Building
- Capital Children's Museum
- Folger Shakespeare Library
- Kenilworth Aquatic Gardens
- Library of Congress
- Lillian Albert Small Jewish Museum
- The Mall
- National Postal Museum
- Sewall-Belmont House
  (National Women's Party Headquarters)
- Supreme Court
- Trailways Bus Station
- Union Station

Capitol Hill

Capitol Hill

What's Nearby

Eastern Market

7th and C Streets SE
Washington, DC

Eastern Market

Hours: Tues-Sat, 7 am - 9 pm;
Sun, 9 am - 4 pm.

This one's a winner – you can learn history by eating! The Eastern Market has been a public food market in Washington since the mid-19th century. And you can still shop here. (The crab cakes are famous.)

Grant Memorial and James Garfield Memorial

1st Street and Maryland Avenue SW
Washington, DC

The Grant sculpture group is the largest in the city – 235 feet long. The Garfield Memorial commemorates our other assassinated president.

A Few Cool Neighborhoods

Lincoln Park

E Capitol Street between 11th and 13th Streets
Washington, DC

Lincoln Park

Metro: Blue, Orange
lines to Capitol South

One of the original parks planned by Pierre L'Enfant, this vest-pocket gem boasts two statues commemorating the African-American struggle: Thomas Ball's "Emancipation Monument," depicting Lincoln freeing the slaves, and Robert Berk's "Bethune Statue," a monument to educator Mary McLeod Bethune.

Navy Museum at the Washington Navy Yard

901 M Street SE
Washington, DC 20374
(202) 433-4882
www.history.navy.mil

Navy Museum at the Washington Navy Yard

Metro: Green line to Navy Yard

Hours: Open *by appointment only* M-F, 9 am - 4 pm; Closed Thanksgiving, Dec 24-25, New Year's Day.

Cost: Free.

Programs like "Hats Off!" and "Dive! Dive!" are aimed at children of different ages as well as adults.

Peace Monument

1st St and Pennsylvania Avenue
Washington, DC 20374

Peace Monument

Metro: Red line to Union Station

A white marble female figure mourning the Navy dead of the Civil War.

Connecticut Avenue

Connecticut Avenue

From near the White House to the Maryland suburbs

Washington Cathedral

Connecticut Avenue is one of the city's longest grand boulevards, stretching up the western edge of Rock Creek Park from just around the corner from the White House all the way out into the far Maryland suburbs and passing through some of the prettiest neighborhoods in the Northwest quadrant of the District. We're looking here at the stretch from Calvert Street NW to Chevy Chase Circle at the border with Maryland.

A particularly well-mannered portion of the city lined with grand hotels and pricey apartment buildings, Connecticut Avenue's small clusters of high-end shopping and stellar restaurants, particularly around Calvert Street NW, Cleveland Park, Van Ness, and Chevy Chase, give parents lots of opportunity to part with their hard-earned cash in a most enjoyable fashion.

For the kids, there's the National Zoo, of course, easily accessible from either Woodley Park or Cleveland Park Metro stops. If you decide to walk up the (definitely steep) hill from Woodley, be sure to look south first, as the enormous lions guarding the Taft Bridge always gave my older daughter a thrill. Another nearby don't-miss stop is the Washington Cathedral, just west of Connecticut Ave on Woodley Road or Cathedral Avenue (a half-mile walk, and also uphill.) Be sure to stop in and ask about the gargoyles.

Connecticut Avenue

Metro: Red Line to Woodley Park-Zoo, Cleveland Park, Van Ness/UDC, Tenley Town/AU, and Friendship Heights

Also in the Neighborhood
• Hillwood Museum & Gardens
• National Zoological Park
• Peirce Mil
• Rock Creek Park
• Washington Dolls' House and Toy Museum

A Few Cool Neighborhoods

What's Nearby

Brazilian-American Cultural Institute

4103 Connecticut Avenue NW
Washington, DC 20008
(202) 382-8334
Metro: Red line to Van Ness/UDC

Art exhibits and concerts of Brazilian works.

The Kennedy-Warren

3133 Connecticut Avenue NW
Washington, DC 20008

The Kennedy-Warren

Metro: Red line to Cleveland Park

Cost: Free

Art Deco private architecture (as opposed to government buildings) is better represented along this stretch of Connecticut Avenue than in most Washington areas. The Kennedy-Warren apartment building is one of the more striking examples.

Washington National Cathedral and Bishop's Gardens

Massachusetts and Wisconsin Avenues NW
Washington, DC 20016
(202) 537-6200
www.cathedral.org/cathedral

The second-largest church in the country, this is the seat of the capital's Episcopal church and has been the place of worship of many Presidents.

Washington National Cathedral and Bishop's Gardens

Metro: Red line to Tenleytown

Hours: Mon-Sat, 10 am - 4:30 pm (extended in summer); Sun, 12:30 - 4:30 pm.

Cost: Donation requested.

Impressive and lovely, the Washington Cathedral

Connecticut Avenue

Downtown

Between M Street NW, 16th Street NW, 22nd Street NW, and Constitution Avenue and the Mall

Hey, it's only the thriving business district of the most powerful city in the world. What's it got? Historic streetscapes and broad avenues, scores of restaurants, the city's newest arts, dining, sports, and entertainment scene, and world-renown theaters, museums, and memorials.

Downtown

Metro: Red line to McPherson Square; Red, Blue, Orange lines to Metro Center; Green, Yellow, Red lines to Gallery Place, Judiciary Square, Federal Triangle, Archives

Forget about Cap Hill and the Mall; this is the city's political, social, commercial, and historic heart. Here you'll find the site of our Old City Hall (right across the street from Daniel Webster's home and office). This is where Walt Whitman nursed Civil War wounded in the former Patent Office, now the National Portrait Gallery. In fact, some 200-odd buildings in the Downtown Historic District carry a historic registry designation, including some stunning architectural examples of Italianate, Romanesque Revival, Gothic Revival, Beaux-Arts, and Classical Revival buildings.

On a more human scale, this is where wave after wave of immigrants from Europe, Asia, and Africa have settled over the decades to create a truly great multicultural city.

And for kids? The list is almost too long! Most kids get a real kick out of Ford's Theatre and the house where Lincoln died. Me, I was a bookish lad, and preferred the Shakespeare Theatre and the Martin Luther King Jr. Memorial Library.

Oh, yeah. This is also the city's entertainment center, boasting several of its most significant theaters and the MCI Center, home of the Wizards (NBA), Mystics (WNBA), Capitals (NHL), a lot of NCAA action, and just about every cool rock band. (At this writing, N-Sync and Paul McCartney are scheduled for the near future.)

A Few Cool Neighborhoods

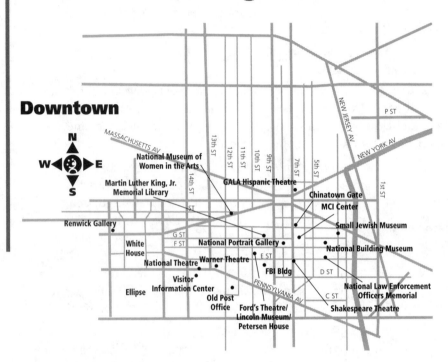

Downtown

Also in the Neighborhood

- FBI Building
- Ford's Theatre/Lincoln Museum
- GALA Hispanic Theatre
- Mary Mcleod Bethune Council House
- MCI Center
- National Building Museum
- National Geographic Explorers Hall
- National Museum of Women in the Arts
- National Portrait Gallery
- National Theatre
- Old Post Office
- Petersen House
- The Shakespeare Theatre
- Smithsonian American Art Museum
- Visitor Information Center of the DC Chamber of Commerce
- Warner Theatre

Downtown

What's Nearby

Chinatown Gateway Arch

7th and H Streets NW
Washington, DC

Chinatown Gateway Arch

Metro: Green, Yellow, Red lines to
Gallery Place/Chinatown

Washington and Beijing are sister cities, and the entry gate into Chinatown was built to evoke that relationship – but it's even larger than any gate in Beijing.

Martin Luther King, Jr. Memorial Library

901 G Street NW
Washington, DC 20001
(202) 727-1111
www.dclibrary.org/mlk

Martin Luther King, Jr. Memorial Library

Metro: Green, Yellow, Red lines to Gallery Place/Chinatown; Red, Blue, Orange lines to Metro Center.

Hours: Mon-Thurs, 10 am - 9 pm; Fri-Sat, 10 am - 5:30 pm; Sun, 1-5 pm.

Opened in 1972, the central branch of the DC public library system was designed by world-famous architect Mies van der Rohe. It's worth a stop just to see the immense mural in the lobby, by artist Don Miller, depicting scenes from the life of Dr. King and the history of the civil rights movement.

National Law Enforcement Officers Memorial

E Street NW between 4th and 5th Streets
Washington, DC

A park honoring the thousands of police officers – city, state, and federal across the nation – killed in the line of duty since 1794.

A Few Cool Neighborhoods

Dupont Circle/Kalorama

North of Downtown, between S Street NW,
Rock Creek Park, 16th Street NW, and L Street

In the center of Dupont Circle, at the intersection
of three major avenues – Connecticut, Massachusetts and New Hampshire –
and several side streets, you'll find one of my favorite hangouts as a young
bohemian. Daniel Chester French's glorious white marble Dupont Memorial
Fountain hosts an interesting crowd: green-haired bike couriers in T-shirts and

Adam T. Lass

Dupont Memorial Fountain

shorts and mothers with strollers
mix with Armani-clad businessmen,
sunbathers, and picnickers. Local
kids play soccer, maybe some chess,
or just glory in a dread-locked
busker's jazzy sax solo.

And that eclectic blend best typi-
fies this cosmopolitan neighborhood. Here you'll find some of the
city's finest museums and historic
homes, as well as an array of ethnic
restaurants, unique bookstores, and
the city's largest concentration of
private art galleries. Like many
bohemian neighborhoods around the country, Dupont Circle has been a center
of Washington's gay life for years. Of particular interest to kids: the National
Geographic Society's Explorer Hall houses an amazing array of permanent and
rotating exhibits, where they can mess with interactive computer kiosks and
"unearth" dinosaurs.

Also in the Neighborhood
• *B'nai Brith Klutznick National Jewish Museum*
• *Heurich House Museum and Historical Society of Washington*
• *National Geographic Society Explorers Hall*
• *Phillips Collection*
• *Society of the Cincinnati Museum at Anderson House*
• *Textile Museum*
• *Woodrow Wilson House*

Dupont Circle/Kalorama

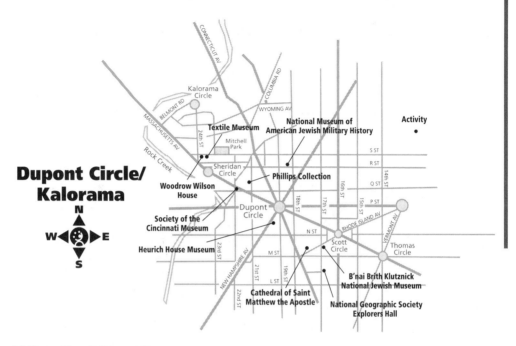

Dupont Circle/ Kalorama

N
W — E
S

What's Nearby

Cathedral of Saint Matthew the Apostle

1725 Rhode Island Avenue NW
Washington, DC 20036
(202) 347-3215
www.stmatthewscathedral.org

> **Cathedral of Saint Matthew the Apostle**
>
> Hours: Sun-Fri, 6:30 am - 6:30 pm; Sat, 7:30 am - 6:30 pm.

The seat of Washington's Catholic bishop, this was where President John F. Kennedy's funeral was held on November 25, 1963. A plaque in front of the main altar commemorates the event.

National Museum of American Jewish Military History

1811 R Street NW
Washington, DC 20009
(202) 265-6280

> **National Museum of American Jewish Military History**
>
> Metro: Red line to Dupont Circle
>
> Hours: M-F, 9 am - 5 pm; Sun, 1-5 pm.
>
> Cost: Free.

From medals and uniforms – even a Confederate uniform – to books and documents, exhibits cover 150 years of participation by American Jews in the nation's wars.

A Few Cool Neighborhoods

East of the River (the Anacostia, that is)

Southeast, north, and south of Pennsylvania Avenue

The Potomac river may be on all the postcards, but Washington, DC, has another river too. It's the Anacostia, and it's got a 1,200-acre riverfront park teeming with wildlife – including bald eagles and beaver – and some glorious views of the capital.

> **East of the River**
> Metro: Orange line
> to Deanwood

All visitors will be rewarded by a trip to this secret side of town (you can get here by crossing the Eleventh Street Bridge, which John Wilkes Booth used to make his escape after assassinating President Lincoln). The Anacostia, and the neighborhood to the east of its banks, are of particular importance to anyone searching out the too-often buried, paved-over, or otherwise obscured aspects of the African-American political and social heritage. I, for one, would rather spend the day exploring Cedar Hill, Frederick Douglass' dignified (and well-preserved) home where the "Sage of Anacostia" wrote his autobiography, than waiting in line to see the Lincoln bedroom again. There's also the Anacostia Museum and Center for African American History and Culture, the

Adam T. Lass

Cedar Hill (F. Douglass National Historic Site)

only branch of the Smithsonian that focuses solely on the identification, documentation, protection, and interpretation of African American history and culture in Washington, DC, and the rural South. And for sheer beauty, you can't beat the Kenilworth Aquatic Gardens, the country's only national park devoted entirely to aquatic plants, with more than 14 acres of ponds and more than 1,000 different species of plants.

Also in the Neighborhood
- *Anacostia Park*
- *Anacostia Museum and Center for African American History and Culture*
- *Frederick Douglass National Historic Site*
- *Kenilworth Aquatic Gardens*
- *RFK Stadium*

East of the River

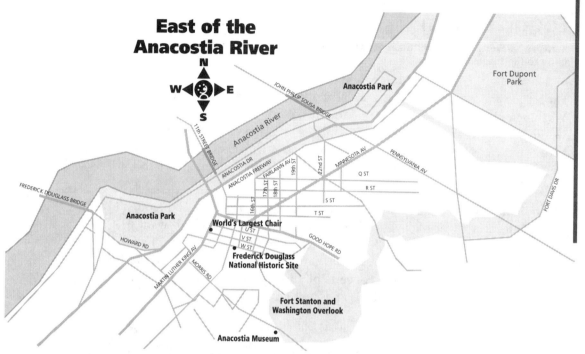

East of the Anacostia River

What's Nearby

Fort Stanton and Washington Overlook

1600 Morris Road SE
Washington, DC 20020

Fort Stanton and Washington Overlook
Hours: Dawn to dusk
Cost: Free

High over the riverfront neighborhood, in a wooded grove next to the parking lot of Our Lady of Perpetual Help Catholic Church, is a plaque marking the site of Fort Stanton, one of the 64 forts that once ringed the capital city. The view of the city from the overlook, 380 feet over the Potomac, is worth seeking out.

World's Largest Chair

V Street and Martin Luther King Jr. Avenue SE
Washington, DC

Kids get a bang out of looking at this 19-foot high solid mahogany chair sitting in a tiny park. A Washington curiosity, it was built in 1959 as a tribute from a furniture manufacturer to a local furniture store.

A Few Cool Neighborhoods

Foggy Bottom

Between Lafayette Square and Georgetown, from south of Dupont Circle to the Potomac

Foggy Bottom

Metro: Blue, Orange lines to Foggy Bottom/GWU

This is another one of those neighborhoods with almost too much on tap. Once a stolid working-class neighborhood, Washington's "West End" was home to Irish, German, and African-American workers at the nearby breweries, glass plants, and the city gas works. Now it's better known as the home of George Washington University, the U.S. State Department, and the Watergate Apartments and Hotel (where a certain burglary took place).

And while the university may offer a vast array of academic, athletic, and entertainment activities for your older kids, the whole family will want to check out the free show at the Kennedy Center's Millennium Stage. For the past four years, tourists and townies have mingled in the Center's Grand Foyer at 6 pm every evening to enjoy concerts of all sorts from classical quartets and opera soloists to romping Dixieland and cool jazz.

Also in the Neighborhood
- Art Museum of the Americas
- The Corcoran
- DAR Constitution Hall
- DAR Museum
- George Washington University
- John F. Kennedy Center for the Performing Arts
- Lisner Auditorium
- The Octagon
- Watergate Apartment-Hotel Complex

Foggy Bottom

What's Nearby

Albert Einstein Memorial

National Academy of Sciences
2101 Constitution Avenue NW
Washington, DC 20418
(202) 334-2436

Albert Einstein Memorial

Metro: Orange, Blue lines
to Foggy Bottom/GWU

An almost-playful Einstein sits over a map of the universe in sculptor Robert Berks' tribute to the great scientist, created to celebrate Einstein's centennial in 1979.

Alexander Pushkin Statue

22nd and H Streets NW
(on George Washington University campus)
Washington, DC

Yet another of Washington's monumental sculptures; this one, by Russian sculptor Alexander Bourganov, is the first in the country honoring a Russian writer.

Benito Juarez Statue

Virginia and New Hampshire Avenues NW
Washington, DC

Along with the Bolivar statue (below), this 1969 statue of 19th-century Mexican revolutionary and president Benito Juarez by Enrique Alciati honors our country's ties with Latin America.

Benito Juarez statue

A Few Cool Neighborhoods

General Simon Bolivar Statue

18th Street and C Street NW
Washington, DC

Adam T. Loss

General Simon Bolivar statue

One of the largest equestrian statues in the country, this 27-foot high tribute to the South American liberator was created by the Felix George Weichs du Weldon, sculptor of the Iwo Jima memorial in Arlington National Cemetery, and donated to Washington by the government of Venezuela in 1959.

Negro Mother and Child Statue

1849 C Street NW (inside courtyard of the Department of the Interior).
Washington, DC 20240

In 1934, in the depths of the Great Depression, the federal Works Project Administration commissioned artists and writers across the country to create significant art for America. This was one such work, a statue of a black woman and child at a time when there were no public sculptures of African-Americans in Washington.

> **Negro Mother and Child Statue**
>
> Hours: Courtyard open dawn to dusk.

Georgetown

Georgetown

**From the Potomac River north to Garfield Street and
Rock Creek Park west to Battery Kemble Park**

Georgetown

The Metro doesn't go to
Georgetown. Take Red line to
Dupont Circle or Orange, Blue
lines to Foggy Bottom, then walk
or take the G2 Georgetown
University bus.

When I grew up in and around Washington, historic Georgetown (it actually predates the rest of the city by 40 years) was our own little Haight-Ashbury, a funky mix of stately old mansions and gorgeous gardens, hippy group houses packed to the rafters with artists and musicians, and peculiar little jewelry shops, galleries, and nightclubs located in cobblestone-paved and gas-lit Victorian back alleyways. The hippies and strange shops are mostly gone, replaced by Prada and Banana Republic. The shopping may be a bit pricey, but it's still awesome, and the architecture is still an eclectic mix of everything from Colonial to Victorian.

As far as kids go, I think Georgetown's best features are both down by the water. Between M Street and the River is the beginning of two of our best parks: Rock Creek Park's hiking and biking trails start here, as does the C&O Canal, where for a modest fee, you can ride a genuine mule-drawn canal boat for an hour and a half. If your kids are the self-powered types (or if you're desperate to wear them out a little), there's the Thompson Boat Center, where you can rent canoes for trips on either the canal or the river (they also rent bikes by the hour and day).

And if you're feeling really bold (and just a bit nostalgic) and want to disabuse your kids of the notion that Wes Craven invented scary movies, you can visit the infamous "Georgetown Steps," a steep and narrow stone staircase between M and L Streets that figured prominently in one of the more gruesome scenes in the movie *The Exorcist*.

Also in the Neighborhood
• *Chesapeake and Ohio Canal*
• *Dumbarton Oaks*
• *Dumbarton House Museum*
• *Georgetown University*
• *Kreeger Museum*
• *Rock Creek Park*

A Few Cool Neighborhoods

What's Nearby

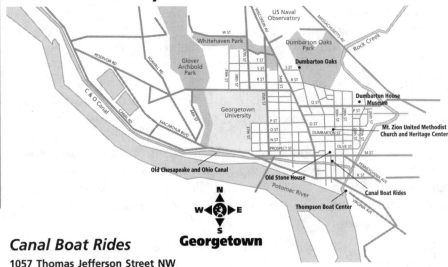

Canal Boat Rides

1057 Thomas Jefferson Street NW
Washington, DC 20007
(202) 653-5190

Mt. Zion United Methodist Church and Heritage Center

1334 29th Street NW
Washington, DC 20037
(202) 234-0148

The oldest African-American church in the city, founded in 1816.

Mt. Zion United Methodist Church and Heritage Center
Hours: By appointment.
Cost: Free.

Old Stone House

3051 M Street NW
Washington, DC 20037
(202) 426-6851

Built in 1765 and possibly the oldest extant building in the city.

Old Stone House
Hours: Wed-Sun, 12-5 pm.
Cost: Free.

Thompson Boat Center

Rock Creek Parkway and V Avenue
Washington, DC 20007
(202) 333-4861

Thompson Boat Center
Bicycle rentals: Mon-Sat, begin at 7:00 am, last rental at 6:00 pm, must be returned by 7:00 pm; Sun, begin at 8:00 am, last rental at 5:00 pm, must be returned by 6:00 pm. Scull rentals are from one hour after opening to two hours prior to closing. Shells need to be returned 45 minutes before closing
Cost: All-terrain bikes: $8/hour, $25/day; one-speed cruisers $4/hour, $15/day. Kayaks (single): $8/hour, $24/day; Kayaks (double): $10/hour, $30/day; canoes (two occupants): $8/hour, $22/day

Georgia Avenue

Georgia Avenue

From Shaw all the way north to the Maryland line

Georgia Avenue

Metro: Green line to
Mount Vernon/UDC,
Shaw/Howard U

We sometimes forget that much of the Civil War was fought literally on Washington DC's doorstep (and in one case, actually crossed that threshold with a real bang). Georgia Avenue's intriguing historic sites are as vivid a reminder as any.

I recommend visiting Fort Stevens, situated about two-thirds of the way up Georgia Avenue. One of a series of 64 forts set up in 1861 to form a protective ring around the capital, Fort Stevens was the only one that actually saw military action. In 1864, its mostly volunteer defenders were attacked (from the north!) by a Confederate force led by General Jubal T. Early. The Battle of Fort Stevens was the closest Confederate troops ever came to capturing the city and the only military action ever to take place in the city – and the only battle in American history directly observed by a sitting President. (Lincoln rode up by carriage to check out the action in person.)

For a more current thrill, you can join folks from all over the mid-Atlantic who come to Georgia Avenue every weekend in June to check out the Caribbean Festival's colorful parade, music, food, and free concerts.

Also in the Neighborhood
- *Howard University*
- *Rock Creek Nature Center*
- *Rock Creek Park Planetarium*

A Few Cool Neighborhoods

What's Nearby

Battleground National Cemetery

6625 Georgia Avenue NW
Washington, DC 20012

The burial place of the 41 Union soldiers who died at the battle of Fort Stevens.

Fort Stevens

13th and Quackenbos Streets
Washington, DC

National Museum of Health and Medicine

Walter Reed Army Medical Center
6900 Georgia Avenue NW
Washington, DC 20012
(202) 782-2200

A museum for the young would-be doctor, complete with live leeches and the bullet that killed President Lincoln.

Battleground National Cemetery

Metro: Green line to U St/Cardozo

Fort Stevens

Metro: Green, Yellow, Blue, Orange lines to L'Enfant Plaza

Hours: Dawn to dusk.

Cost: Free.

National Museum of Health and Medicine

Hours: Daily, 10 am - 5:30 pm; reservations and picture ID required; Closed Dec 25.

Cost: Free.

Lafayette Square

Lafayette Square

Right in front of the White House on Pennsylvania Avenue

Lafayette Square

Metro: Blue, Orange lines to
Farragut West, McPherson Square

The first thing you're going to notice about Lafayette Square is that it's right across the street from the White House. But like so much else about Washington, there's a good bit more to it than that. Named to honor the French general who rode to our defense at a critical moment during the Revolutionary War, this square across the street from 1600 Pennsylvania Avenue was once the most chic address in the city. When John and Abigail Adams moved into the (still unfinished and, to be honest, quite drafty) White House, the most elegant and powerful people of our relatively new nation made their homes in the lovely townhouses that surround the park, to be close to the center of action. (Remember, in those days, you couldn't just pick up a phone and call the White House. The ability to drop in on the President didn't just indicate prestige and personal power; it was political power itself.)

At this writing, Lafayette Square is about as close as you or I can get the White House. But you can certainly visit the many historic homes and major museums – from the Octagon to Decatur House to St. John's Church, the church of the Presidents – that surround it.

And while those sites will certainly thrill older, more historically minded youths, my kids always seemed most to enjoy Lafayette Park itself, with its tree-shaded paths and intriguing statues. (A note to remember on hot Washington days: For some reason, this square always seems a little cooler than the surrounding city.)

Also in the Neighborhood
• Art Museum of the Americas
• The Corcoran
• Daughters of the American Revolution Museum
• Decatur House Museum
• The Octagon Museum
• Renwick Gallery of the Smithsonian American Art Museum
• The White House

A Few Cool Neighborhoods

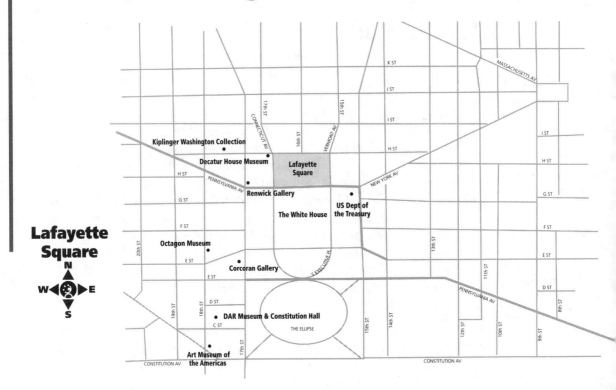

What's Nearby

The Kiplinger Washington Collection

1729 H Street NW
Washington, DC 20006
(202) 887-6537

The Kiplinger Washington Collection
Hours: By appointment only.

5,000 paintings, drawings, and photographs of Washington architecture. The collection of the same W.M. Kiplinger who created the famous financial newsletter.

U.S. Department of the Treasury

1500 Pennsylvania Avenue NW
Washington, DC 20020
(202) 622-0896

The third-oldest government building in Washington, dating to 1869, and home to a key part of the world's most powerful economy. Not open to the public at this writing.

Sixteenth Street Corridor

Sixteenth Street Corridor

From the White House and Pennsylvania Avenue north to the Maryland line

Sixteenth Street Corridor

Metro: Blue, Orange lines to Farragut West, McPherson Square

16th Street may start with the world's most important address, but it doesn't end there. In reality, it's another of Washington, DC's stately boulevards. Queen Anne, Italianate, Richardsonian Romanesque, and Beaux-Arts homes sit just off its tree-lined lanes as it runs in a straight line all the way to Silver Spring, Maryland.

Here's just a few things that you won't want to miss. Turn your back on the White House and walk up a couple of blocks and there's the Russian Embassy just off M Street. I can't be the only kid who grew up thinking that that brooding gothic façade was intriguing and romantic. I just knew that if I watched long enough, I could see a real spy walk right through the front door bold as could be.

Slightly more "normal" kids will want to check out Meridian Hill Park (AKA Malcolm X Park), with its thrilling cascading waterfall and statues dedicated to such exotic notables as Joan of Arc and Dante.

Also in the Neighborhood
- Scottish Rite Temple and Supreme Council Library
- Meridian Hill/Malcolm X Park
- Heurich House
- Carter-Barron Amphitheater

A Few Cool Neighborhoods

What's Nearby

Carnegie Institute of Washington

1530 P Street NW
Washington, DC 20005
(202) 939-1142

The Institute is for the advancement of science, but it's the building that's interesting to visitors. A stunning Art-Moderne mansion built in 1910, it's one of those places that prompt kids to ask, "People *lived* here?"

District of Columbia Jewish Community Center

1529 16th Street NW
Washington, DC 20036
(202) 518-9400

Once and again a center of Jewish life in Washington, the center offers arts programs and exhibits, performances, and gym facilities.

Mexican Cultural Institute

2829 16th Street NW
Washington, DC 20009
(202) 728-1628

Exhibits of Mexican art and performances of Mexican music in the former Mexican embassy.

Mexican Cultural Institute

Hours: Open Tues-Sat 11 am - 5 pm.

Cost: Admission free

Southwest

Southwest

From the Mall south to Hain's Point, where the Anacostia flows into the Potomac

Southwest

Metro: Green, Yellow, Blue,
Orange lines to L'Enfant
Plaza, Federal Ctr, Waterfront

Another "forgotten" (translate as, "the locals know it and tourists don't") part of town, Southwest is the smallest quadrant of the city – and well worth visiting. In fact, it was once known around town as "the Island," because it was surrounded on two sides by the Potomac and Anacostia Rivers and cut off from the rest of DC on the third side by the old Washington Canal, now better known as Constitution Avenue. (You can still see a Gatekeepers House at 17th and Constitution Avenue).

Today it is still an active waterfront community and host to DC's historic Fish Wharf, with lots of restaurants replete with river views (seafood is the cuisine of choice, naturally) and plenty of boating activity.

Like many other less famous parts of DC, Southwest has a rich working-class heritage. A former stop on the Underground Railroad, this was always the sort of neighborhood where a rabbi's son like Al Jolson could pick up his blues singer's chops just playing on the street. Remnants of the Old Southwest still peek through after decades of renovation. Not far from the waterfront, you'll find St. Dominic's Church and Wheat Row, the earliest row houses built in Washington.

But highest on this neighborhood's don't-miss list is the Arena Stage. One of the nation's first repertory theaters, it made Washington history in1951 when it began holding performances for integrated audiences, breaking with nearly a century of bleak Washington tradition. There's almost always something brewing here for kids on one or another of its smaller stages.

Also in the Neighborhood
• *Arena Stage*

A Few Cool Neighborhoods

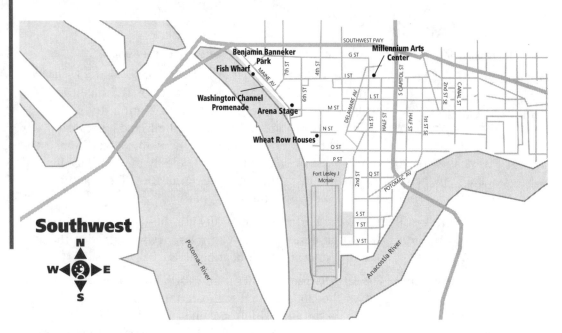

What's Nearby

Benjamin Banneker Park

10th and G Streets SW
Washington, DC

A waterfront park named for the surveyor who was one of the country's first black engineers.

Fish Wharf

1100 Maine Avenue SW
Washington, DC 20024

One of the best spots in Washington for seafood.

Benjamin Banneker Park

Metro: Green, Yellow, Blue, Orange lines to L'Enfant Plaza

Fish Wharf

Metro: Green line to Waterfront

Southwest

Millennium Arts Center

65 Eye Street SW
Washington, DC 20024
(202) 479-2573
www.millenniumartscenter.org

This huge space provides work space and exhibit space for artists working in a wide range of arts, from sculpture to glass blowing.

Millennium Arts Center

Metro: Green line to Waterfront

Wheat Row

1315 - 1321 4th Street SW
Washington, DC 20024

The first row houses built in Washington, dating to 1794.

Wheat Row

Metro: Green line to Waterfront

Washington Channel Promenade

at the end of Maine Avenue on the waterfront

A pleasant walk along the water brings you to a park with a monument to the victims of the *Titanic* sinking.

Washington Channel Promenade

Metro: Green line to Waterfront

A Few Cool Neighborhoods

U Street/Shaw

U Street NW between 7th and 16th Streets

Before there was the Harlem renaissance or the Apollo Theatre, there was Duke Ellington's hometown Shaw, where big-time entertainers, black-owned businesses, and grand movie theaters made U Street the place to be and to be seen.

In the 1860s, a steady flow of freedmen escaping oppression further South found shelter in the area (many of the mission churches they founded still hold services today). That strong and vibrant black culture was further bolstered in the 1870s, when Howard University began to attract the nation's black intellectual and artistic leadership.

By the early 20th century, Shaw was a bustling center of the city's black community, replete with businesses, clubs, theatres, and the major social institutions of black Washington. In fact, it was the largest urban African-American community in the nation until Harlem surpassed it in the '20s.

I regularly attend and highly recommend the Smithsonian Jazz Orchestra's free shows at the Lincoln theatre. Another really cool place to visit is the Black Fashion Museum, where you can see exhibits of antique and recent garments along with memorabilia that illustrate critical black contributors to the fashion industry, like Elizabeth Keckley, the first "known" black dressmaker to sew for a President's wife (Mary Todd Lincoln), and Ann Lowe, who designed Jackie Kennedy's wedding gown.

U Street/Shaw

Metro: Green line to U St/Cardozo or Shaw-Howard Univ.

Landmarks abound on U Street/Shaw

Also in the Neighborhood
• *Mary McLeod Bethune Council House National Historic Site*
• *Studio Theatre*

U Street/Shaw

U Street/ Shaw

What's Nearby

African American Civil War Memorial

1200 U Street NW
Washington, DC 20001
(202) 667-2667

African American Civil War Memorial

Metro: Green line to U St/Cardozo or Shaw-Howard Univ

The 200,000 African-American troops of the Civil War didn't get a memorial for more than a century. Then, in 1998, Washington finally put up this sculpture by Ed Hamilton in the heart of historic U Street-Shaw.

Black Fashion Museum

2007 Vermont Avenue NW
Washington, DC 20001
(202) 667-0744
www.bfmdc.org

Black Fashion Museum

Metro: Green line to U St/Cardozo

Hours: Open by appointment only.

Cost: Suggested Donation, $2.

The achievements of African-Americans – like Ann Lowe, who designed for First Lady Jackie Kennedy – in the world of fashion.

A Few Cool Neighborhoods

Duke Ellington Mural

1214 U Street NW
Washington, DC 20009

A huge likeness of the great African-American jazz composer by artist G. Byron Peck. The mural is on the side of Mood Indigo, a second-hand clothes and memorabilia shop named for one of Ellington's most famous compositions.

Duke Ellington Mural

Metro: Green line to U St/African-American Civil War Memorial

HR57 Center for the Preservation of Jazz and Blues

1610 14th Street NW
Washington, DC 20009
(202) 667-3700

A performance space and an archive of jazz and blues history. Younger children, particularly those not interested in jazz and blues might prefer that you to choose another venue to entertain them, but older aficionados should appreciate a performance here.

HR57 Center for the Preservation of Jazz and Blues

Metro: Green line to U St/African-American Civil War Memorial

Hours: Wed, Fri, and Sat evenings.

Lincoln Theatre

1215 U Street NW
Washington, DC 20009
(202) 328-9177
www.thelincolntheatre.org

Washington's answer to Harlem's famed Apollo Theater.

Lincoln Theatre

Bethesda, MD

Over the Border

No description of the locales of the DC area would be complete without covering four of the places that are outside the city limits, but are still fully integrated threads in DC's social fabric.

Bethesda, Maryland

Wisconsin Avenue between the District line and the Beltway

Glen Echo Park, Bethesda

Adam T. Loss

> **Bethesda, Maryland**
>
> Metro: Red line to Bethesda, Medical Center, Grosvenor

I confess; I am not a DC native. Rather, I grew up in what was a sleepy little suburb just across the DC line. In those days, if you wanted to do anything interesting at all on a Saturday night, you got on a bus heading south down Wisconsin Avenue.

Now that weekend traffic flow has reversed itself in a big way. Bethesda has blossomed over the past three decades into a major restaurant Mecca, with restaurants featuring almost any cuisine you can imagine.

Money No Object?

La Miche

905 Norfolk Avenue
Bethesda, MD
(301) 986-0707

If you want classic French food, Bethesda can compete with Paris. This is where I go with *my* dad on those big round-number birthdays for roast lamb and puff pastries. For two decades, its cozy dining room has evoked the best of the French countryside, with baskets hanging from the ceiling and provincial furniture. The menu is long, and the list of daily specials is longer.

A Few Cool Neighborhoods

Ruth's Chris Steak House

7315 Wisconsin Avenue
Bethesda, MD
(301) 652-7877

If big thick juicy steaks is more your game, forget about Outback and pull up a chair for perfectly aged inch-thick beauties.

Tragara Ristorante

4935 Cordell Avenue
Bethesda, MD
(301) 951-4935

I can think of no better way to spend a couple hundred bucks lunching among the well-heeled. The appetizers alone are worth the wad you will drop here: pepperoni in padella, warm sweet red peppers cooked with garlic, capers and olives; baked stuffed artichokes dressed with olive oil, garlic, bits of olive and capers. Or maybe the sampler that combines spinach agnolotti in a cream sauce with capellini in a fresh tomato sauce (excuse me, I need to mop my chin a bit).

Back To Reality

Ahh, back to reality. No I can't eat at these places more than once or twice a year either. But Bethesda hosts plenty of fine eateries for more modest budgets as well. Here are few of my favorites:

Bacchus

7945 Norfolk Avenue
Bethesda, MD
(301) 657-1722

Bacchus features a stunning list of Lebanese mezze: tangy sausages, fragrant vegetable dishes and sesame-flavored dips, deft versions of the familiar hummus, baba ghanouj and such, followed by intense kebabs of lamb, chicken or fish, grilled to a charred and juicy state.

Bethesda, MD

Black's Bar & Kitchen

7750 Woodmont Avenue
Bethesda, MD
(301) 652-6278

Be sure to check out the impressive catch of the day. Start with "New Orleans chopped salad," juicy fried crayfish tails and kicky Creole dressing, or shrimp sporting a nubby coat of plantain, delicious with its mango-melon salsa. For dinner, I recommend the tuna with grilled pineapple and cilantro-lime vinaigrette or the wondrous crisp-edged duck breast with haricots verts, creamy grits and a mustardy moistener.

Cafe Deluxe

4910 Elm Street
Bethesda, MD
(301) 656-3131

The first time I stepped in with my two-year-old daughter under one arm and a diaper bag, sippy cup and Elmo balanced under the other, I was immediately relieved to see a virtual peaceable kingdom: couples with small children, (all of whom were surprisingly well-behaved) happily sitting amongst older couples, black spectacled laptop geeks, well-dressed women execs, and neo-Italian hipsters. The menu is varied, and some of its least innovative dishes are its most popular. The meatloaf, or herb-roasted chicken can put a smile on any young face, while the grilled salmon, a good tuna "mignon" with green pepper sauce and pan-roasted sea bass cut thick enough to be moist, but not so thick that it stays raw inside, pleases older patrons. On a vegetarian diet? I recommend the gazpacho and red pepper hummus rolls or the angel-hair pomodoro and vegetable pizza.

Jaleo-Bethesda

7271 Woodmont Avenue
Bethesda, MD
(301) 913-0003

Mmmm, tapas. Jaleo-Bethesda has over 50 of those wonderfully spicy Spanish finger-food treats. How about scallops in romesco: a blend of onions, tomato, garlic, vinegar, ground almonds, fried bread and sweet peppers . . . or octopus with paprika . . . or date and bacon fritters . . . or anchoas de l'Escala y pan con tomate. The upside: Not one of Jaleo's executive chef Jose Ramon Andres' amazing concoctions has ever failed to thrill me. The downside: Both the downtown and Bethesda Jaleo locations are all the rage, so we're talking about major lines and crowds.

151

A Few Cool Neighborhoods

Chipotle-Bethesda

7600 Old Georgetown Road
Bethesda, MD
(301) 907-9077

The latest entry in the chain burrito joint wars, Chipotle has that little Chihuahua dog's place beat hands down. We're talking fast, clean, and impervious to kids. Huge burritos, quesadillas, and fajitas are custom built right in front of you from the freshest ingredients and served in an ultra cool atmosphere. Oh, and it's way cheap, especially if the younger kids split something.

Original Pancake House

7700 Wisconsin Avenue
Bethesda, MD
(301) 986-0285

Last on my list (but not last in town by long shot – only space considerations prevent me from rattling on for pages) the Original Pancake house features, well, really good pancakes served at least 17 ways, with all the usual berries, nuts and sweets, ranging in price from $2.75 to $7.50. I've had folks in from "pancake country" (AKA rural Ohio) who gave these high praise indeed. "Almost, not quite, but *almost* as good as Mom's." They also offer more appropriate lunch fare, like omelets, soups, sandwiches, and salads.

What's Nearby

The Capital Crescent Trail

Along Potomac River from west end of K Street (beneath Whitehurst Freeway)
past Maryland border to Silver Spring
(301) 492-6245
www.washdc.org/trail1.html

> **The Capital Crescent Trail**
>
> Metro: Orange, Blue lines to Foggy Bottom, Red line to Bethesda

There are few remaining aspects left of the Bethesda of my youth. The soda fountain at the old drugstore is now a multi-story office building, and the pool hall where I swept up after school in exchange for free table time and a lesson or two from the regulars is a Persian rug shop.

These may or may not be improvements. What is a pretty wonderful improvement is what they did to the old Baltimore and Ohio tracks that ran through the center of town. The 11-mile railroad line that carried coal and building supplies on a weekly train to Georgetown until service was discontinued in 1985 has been

Glen Echo Park

incorporated into the Capital Crescent Trail. This beautiful, tree-lined, 10-to-14-foot-wide paved hiker/biker trail passes through parks and other wooded areas, over four historic bridges, and through two historic tunnels, and provides beautiful vistas over the Potomac. It connects with a number of other trails, including the C&O Canal Towpath and the Rock Creek Trail, which together form a 22-mile loop of almost unbroken quiet and joyous green.

Glen Echo Park

George Washington Memorial Parkway
Glen Echo, MD 20812
www.nps.gov/glec

Glen Echo Park
Carousel

Another haunt of my childhood is the former amusement park out in Glen Echo. Glen Echo Park was founded in 1891 as a National Chautauqua Assembly "to promote liberal and practical education, especially among the masses of the people; to teach the sciences, arts, languages, and literature; to prepare its patrons for their several pursuits and professions in life; and to fit them for the duties which devolve upon them as members of society."

By the early 1900s, it had become Washington's own Coney Island. Local families would escape the summer heat with a trolley ride north for a day riding the carousel, roller coaster and bumper cars, plinking ducks at the shooting gallery, or perhaps swimming in the Crystal Pool. Evenings were for dancing in the Spanish Ballroom or sitting with your girl listening to swing bands in the Cuddle Up.

Candy Corner
and Original
Chatauqua Tower

The park fell into serious disrepair and decay in the '60s. It was almost torn down to make way for a housing development, but it was saved by a coalition of local artists and historical preservation buffs, who convinced the National Park Service to adopt it.

Today the park has come full circle. The land and historic buildings are once again the backdrop for a rich arts education program, with year-round activities in dance, theater, and the arts for the surrounding communities and for visitors from across the country. The park also administers an artist-in-residency program that provides the public with an opportunity to see artists at work. There are concerts, demonstrations, workshops, and festivals during the warm months as a part of the Chautauqua Summer season.

A Few Cool Neighborhoods

A Pair of Glen Echo Park Secrets

The Adventure Theatre and Puppet Co.

7300 MacArthur Blvd
Glen Echo, MD
(301) 320-5331

A simple little theater stuffed into the old penny arcade behind the shooting gallery, was a particular favorite of mine in my teen years, when I worked behind the scenes building sets and hanging lights.

I grew to love it all over again as a parent watching my daughter scramble about on its kid-friendly, carpet-covered, Roman-style benches and then stare in rapt attention as costumed actors and puppets played out their own special versions of classic children's tales and fables (but always with a quirky twist to keep mom and dad and older sibs interested too). Adventure Theatre is open year-round, with four performances each weekend. Shows run about 45 minutes and stay in production for about a month. A caveat: Seating is first come-first served, and while there are no bad seats in a hall this small, if you want to be up front, get in line early. A nice touch: The cast members wait in the lobby after each show to sign programs.

The Discovery Creek Children's Museum

7300 MacArthur Blvd
Glen Echo, MD
(202) 364-3111

Another gem is hiding in the park's old stables. This museum offers a continuing series of enjoyable (and educational too, but if you don't tell your kids, I won't) programs on everything from fossil collecting to ant behavior to aquatic animals. Visitors to the city would probably be most interested in the museum's weekend sessions, which include guided and self-guided hikes, Children's Garden scavenger hunts, live animal encounters, exhibitions, discovery backpacks, and special guest appearances. The weekend sessions run from 10 am to 3 pm on Saturdays, and from 11 am to 3 pm on Sundays, each weekend from mid-January through the end of May and in July and August. Discovery Creek is not part of the Smithsonian, unlike so many of the museums in the DC area, so it isn't free, but at $4 a head, admission is cheap enough for any budget.

In addition, the antique hand-carved and hand-painted Dentzel carousel, saved by community effort, operates four days a week from May through September, and the Gallery/Bookshop features park artists in its exhibits.

Takoma Park

Takoma Park

Straddling the District/Maryland Line from Georgia Avenue to New Hampshire Avenue.

Takoma Park

Metro: Red line to Takoma

Remember those hippies who used to live in Georgetown in the 1960s? Well, they all moved to Takoma Park. Attracted like moths to its pleasant lanes and flower-lined yards, they filled its lovely old Victorian houses and Craftsman bungalows and opened one of the oldest food co-ops in the area.

And then they grew up, joined its PTAs and civic associations, and elected themselves to the local board. Now Takoma Park is one of the funkiest and coolest little towns on the East Coast (think Ann Arbor and you've just about got it).

Cool, Off-beat Carroll Avenue

Takoma Park (aka Azalea City) is an official "Tree City, USA," has an award-winning recycling program and supports the work of historic preservation groups. It is a sanctuary city and a nuclear-free zone. It's so liberal here, residents who are not yet U.S. citizens may vote in local elections and hold local elective office.

But TP is more than just a political movement. That's right, it's got shopping too! In fact, it's got all those cool off-beat little shops that used to be in Georgetown. You can find anything here: Tibetan singing bowls, herbal tea, Buddha icons and really hip clothes; Asian furniture and antiques and more hip clothes; vintage purses, bags and pins, old Simplicity/Butterick patterns; and fancy bar glasses, go-go boots, a floating amoeba ashtray and a poodle skirt.

A Few Cool Neighborhoods

House of Musical Traditions

7040 Carroll Ave.
Takoma Park, MD 20912
(301) 270-9090
www.hmtrad.com

House of Musical Traditions

Metro: Red line to Takoma Park

Hours: Tues-Sat, 11 am - 7 pm;
Sun-Mon, 11 am - 5 pm; Closed
July 4, Thanksgiving, Dec 25,
New Year's Day.

Here's my own favorite. David Eisner's House of Musical Traditions has been supporting the local music scene for my entire adult life, with something for any musical taste (ok, a head-banger might get bored there, but anyone into acoustic instruments will be in hog heaven). I have spent many hours exploring their shelves, playing with everything from guitars and accordions to tongue drums and congas. I have never heard them fail to answer a question with genuine enthusiasm, joy, and expertise no matter how professional or amateur the query. And there is still a Beat Jam every Friday night from 8 pm until 10 pm above the store.

Speaking of Dave, you'll find him all over the various stages at the annual Takoma Park Folk Festival in late September. There are several stages of free music of all sorts, dancing lessons, clowns, street performers, exotic ethnic food vendors, and craft stands.

Best yet during the Festival, there's the Grassy Nook Stage for activities designed for children of all ages, with folksingers, interactive musical games and dancing, storytelling, and participatory music-making (with any luck, you will get to hear multiple-Grammy nominees Cathy Fink and Marcy Marxer there, two local treasures who will forever redefine kids' music for you). Nearby are children's homemade games provided by Cub Scout Pack 33 and participatory crafts provided by

the Earth Center for the Arts. This has been a must-attend event for my family for decades. It's almost worth timing your visit to catch it. For more info, check it out on line at **www.tpff.org** or call them at (301) 589-3717.

Adam T. Lass

Alexandria, VA

Alexandria

Virginia side of Potomac River Virginia side of the river from 14th Street Bridge to the Beltway
http://ci.alexandria.va.us

Now would be a good time to get out your regional map. Note that DC is roughly diamond-shaped, *except for that big chunk on the Virginia side of the Potomac.* That chunk is now called Alexandria and Arlington, and it used to be part of DC too, but was ceded back to Virginia in 1847.

Well, they may be on the wrong side of the river, but they're still an important part of town and well worth a visit, especially if your youngsters are starting to get museum-shy. Oh, they've got more than their fair share of fascinating historical spots – with all the places that have "George Washington and Robert E. Lee slept here" placards, you'd think that neither one had a waking moment in his life – but Virginia is also where the great outdoors gets back into the picture in a big way.

This is real Who's Who territory. George Washington, George Mason, and Robert E. Lee are just a few of the big names who lent a hand putting this port city on the map. But its history predates Washington's by a good bit. In 1669, Scotsman John Alexander purchased the land of present-day Alexandria from an English ship captain for "six thousand pounds of Tobacco and Cask." By the time it was incorporated in 1749, Alexandria was a bustling seaport with brigs and schooners in from Europe and the Caribbean waiting in line to belly up to the docks. In 1796, the Duc de La Rochfoucauld Liancourt described Alexandria as "beyond all comparison the handsomest town in Virginia – indeed is among the finest in the United States."

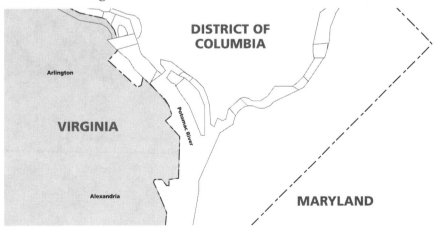

A Few Cool Neighborhoods

Everyone remembers the revolutionary patriots of Boston and Concord. But did you know that Alexandria was also a major center of dissent before the war? On April 14, 1755, a twenty-year period of civil unrest in the colonies began when British General Edward Braddock and five Royal Governors recommended a tax on "all his Majesty's dominions in America" – the first of its kind – to fund the British military campaigns of the French and Indian War. In response to the unfair levy, prominent local leaders (do names like George Washington and George Mason ring a bell?) met at the Court House in Alexandria on July 18, 1774, and adopted Mason's Fairfax Resolves calling for an end to trade with England. Two years later, the country was at war, and the rest as they say, is history.

Alexandria

Metro: Yellow, Blue lines to Braddock, King Street, Van Dorn

Modern Alexandria is a great place to visit, live, and work. It still retains the character and charm of a historic port city and is ranked as the fifth best "Big City for Doing Business" in the U.S. and first in the rankings of the "Best Cities for Women" by the *Ladies' Home Journal*. In fact, it was the only jurisdiction to receive a perfect score for quality of life in the magazine's listing of top 10 cities nationwide.

Adam T. Lass

Alexandria, VA

So it's a great place to see old stuff. But I promised you outdoors, so here are some 50-odd miles of hiking and biking trails to stretch your legs on:

Alexandria Heritage Trail

Alexandria Archaeology
(703) 838-4399

A 22-mile urban trail leads you past more than 40 museums and historic parks where you and your family can learn about Native Americans, Colonists, African Americans, Civil War civilians, and soldiers.

Mount Vernon Forest Trail

(703) 780-2000

A walk through wilderness George Washington would still recognize leads you past mature oak and hickory trees, holly and laurel shrubs and Washington's own cobble quarry.

Mount Vernon Trail

Free map available at the Ramsay House Visitors Center
221 King Street
Alexandria, VA 22314

This 18.5-mile trail follows the banks of the Potomac from George Washington's Mount Vernon Estate and Gardens to Theodore Roosevelt Island. Don't miss the side trips to the Dyke Marsh wildlife habitat or the 19th-century lighthouse at Jones Point Park. Beyond Alexandria, you can check out a sweet vista of the Washington skyline from Gravelly Point and the big wave and gulls sculpture at the Navy-Marine Memorial.

Wheel Nuts

302 Montgomery Street
Alexandria, VA
(703) 548-5116

Don't feel like walking? Stop in for bike rentals by the hour and the day, as well as accessories and repairs.

Also in the Neighborhood

- *Athenaem*
- *DEA Museum*
- *Fort Ward Museum & Historic Site*
- *Gadsby's Tavern Museum*
- *Lyceum*
- *Mount Vernon Estate and Gardens*
- *Ronald Reagan National Airport*
- *Stabler-Leadbeater Apothecary*

A Few Cool Neighborhoods

Atlantic Canoe & Kayak Co

1201 N Royal Street
Alexandria, VA
(800) 297-0066

If you're feeling adventurous and ready for a unique view of the area, consider canoe tours of the Dyke Marsh Wildlife Area, Piscataway Creek, Pohick Bay, Georgetown Monuments & Bridges, Sunset Tours, Moonlight Tours, and the annual 4th of July Fireworks. The short trips are especially good for first-time kayakers, with a brief lesson and all the equipment you'll need.

Cameron Run Regional Park

4001 Eisenhower Avenue
Alexandria, VA
(703) 960-0767

Want your water a little tamer? This park offers something for everyone – waterslide, wave pool, lap pool, batting cages, and miniature golf.

Arlington County

Virginia side of Potomac River from Chain Bridge to the 14th Street Bridge

Arlington County

Metro: Orange line to Rosslyn, Court House, Clarendon, Virginia Square, Ballston, East Falls Church, Arlington Cemetery, Pentagon, Pentagon City, Crystal City, National Airport

You've seen a lot of Arlington. You've seen images of the Pentagon, the U.S. Marine Memorial (the guys in helmets raising the flag over Iwo Jima), Fort Myer, and Arlington National Cemetery in the nightly news, as well as a hundred movies and TV shows, like *Deep Impact* with Tea Leoni and Robert Duvall, *No Way Out* with Kevin Costner, and Francis Ford Coppola's *Gardens of Stone*. *The Scarecrow and Mrs. King* TV series was largely filmed in and around Arlington, and Chris Carter has found it an irresistible setting for many of his spooky midnight meetings in *The X Files*.

Also in the Neighborhood
- *Arlington National Cemetery*
- *Arlington House-Robert E. Lee Memorial*
- *Drug Enforcement Agency Museum*
- *The Pentagon*
- *Reagan National Airport*
- *United States Marine Memorial ("Iwo Jima Memorial")*
- *Women in Military Service for America Memorial*
- *Dulles Airport*

Arlington, VA

The Arlington Historical Society

1805 S Arlington Ridge Road
Arlington, VA
(703) 892-4204

This lovely inner suburb's real claim to fame is its history and the society's museum has more than 350,000 artifacts on rotating display at the two historical landmarks it owns and operates: the oldest existing schoolhouse in the county – a little red-brick building dating back to 1891, complete with bell tower, and the county's oldest standing structure, the Ball-Setters House, built of logs in 1750.

And the Society's exhibits go back a lot further than that. 12,000 years ago, Native Americans occupied more than a dozen sites in Arlington. Your kids probably think Capt. John Smith was just a character in a Disney movie. Well, in 1608, Smith recorded the first encounter with the Nocostins tribe. The tribe's village was on Analostan Island, better known now as Theodore Roosevelt Island.

From 1801 to 1846, Arlington was actually part of the nation's capital, until the federal government approved the return of the county to Virginia. (The street layout and house numbering system still match up with DC's.) The Civil War transformed Arlington County, as it did so much else around the DC area, as 100,000 Union troops were stationed at 22 forts and other encampments to defend the federal capital from Confederate attacks. By 1863, newly emancipated slaves found sanctuary at Freedman's Village in Arlington Heights. (Aspects of this village of more than 100 homes are re-created at the museum.)

Modern Arlington's location just across the Potomac offers visitors relief from urban congestion while still allowing easy access to DC's museums and attractions. In fact, most Arlington hotels are located within four miles of the Smithsonian Institution, the White House, and the U.S. Capitol. It's just a short drive to Mount Vernon, Old Town Alexandria, Potomac Mills outlet mall, Manassas battlefield, and many other Virginia attractions.

And it's got a bunch of local activities to keep your kids busy too, including more than 36 miles of hiking and biking trails and 50 miles of connecting bike routes. (For more information, contact Arlington County Department of Public Works, (703) 228-3681.)

A Few Cool Neighborhoods

Upton Hill Regional Park Mini Golf Course
Wilson Boulevard and Patrick Henry Drive
Arlington, VA

Want to swing a club or two? Test your skill with a putter on the longest mini-golf hole in the world (130 feet). Designed by Jim Bryant, the foremost designer of miniature golf courses in the world, the course is open daily from Memorial Day to Labor Day, and weekends during the spring and fall.

Classika Theatre Studio
2772 S Arlington Mill Drive
Arlington, VA

Here's an odd item that you won't find elsewhere. Since its 2000 inauguration, over 500 children have enjoyed creative classes in the visual and the dramatic arts. This award winning studio's Family Series offers original productions for elementary, middle school students, and family audiences while Classika's Green Parrot Puppet Theatre features puppet and marionette musicals for family audiences.

What's Nearby

Wolf Trap Foundation for the Performing Arts
1624 Trap Road
Vienna, VA 22182
(703) 255-1900
www.wolf-trap.org

Wolf Trap Foundation for the Performing Arts
Metro: Orange line to West Falls Church

"America's National Park for the Performing Arts," Wolf Trap is operated as a public-private partnership between the National Park Service and the Wolf Trap Foundation. It has two venues, an outdoor performance space, the Filene Center, and an indoor theater, the Barns at Wolf Trap, and is home to the Wolf Trap Opera Company.

4 Further Afield: Day Trips

Baltimore

Baltimore

This trip is about 38 miles and takes about an hour. There will be a little zig-zagging in the beginning to get around one of Washington's endless squares. Stay the course and you'll get there just fine. Starting from the White House at 1600 Pennsylvania Ave. NW...

- Head east on H St. NW towards Madison Pl. NW.
- After four blocks, bear left onto New York Ave NW.
- After another four blocks, you'll hit Mt. Vernon Square: bear right onto K St. NW. As you pass the square, K St. will magically turn into Massachusetts Ave NW. This is okay.
- Go one block on Massachusetts and then turn left onto 6th St NW/US-1/US-50.
- After two blocks, turn right onto New York Ave. NW/US-50. Congratulations: the hard part is over.
- Stay on New York Avenue/US-50 for about 3 3/4 miles of truly ugly industrial American landscape till you get to MD-295.
- Get on MD-295 heading toward Baltimore and stay on for about 31 miles. Along the way you'll pass both the Washington Beltway (I-95) and the Baltimore Beltway (I-695).
- As you approach downtown Baltimore, MD-295 will turn into Russell St. This is okay.
- If you are looking for the Inner Harbor, take Russell St. past PSINET Stadium (home of the NFL Baltimore Ravens) and Camden Yards (MLB Baltimore Orioles) to West Pratt St.
- Turn right on Pratt St., drive eight blocks, and you're there.

Please note that this route is also a great way to get to the East and North side of the Washington Beltway and I-95 heading north.

While the immediate DC area is rich in historical sites (some might say overly so) and activities for tourists, there is another Maryland, one that the locals know but doesn't show up in many of the guidebooks, a real Maryland that can offer a visitor a rich, rewarding experience unlike any other.

Let's start with DC's sister city, Baltimore. Location is everything as they say, and this working-class dock town lies farther west than any other major Atlantic port, making its harbor a popular choice for shippers since 1600. In fact, Baltimore is now the fourth-ranked port on the U.S. east coast, with more than 40,000,000 tons of cargo passing through the port every year.

Day Trips

By the early 1800s, Baltimore was growing fast, with a population of almost 50,000 working in support of the harbor as sailmakers, ironworkers, shipwrights, and merchants. This growth and prosperity was about to suffer a serious interruption, but Baltimore's loss was to be the country's gain.

France and Great Britain, at war with one another again, had set up economic blockades to keep each other from getting important supplies. As a neutral carrier for both countries, American merchant ships were frequently caught up in the blockades, their cargos seized (the British, still smarting over the recent loss of the colonies, made a habit of drafting American sailors into the Royal Navy).

Between the blockades and seizures, British agitation of Native Americans on the Western frontier, and a long list of additional provocations, the United States declared war on Great Britain in June 1812 to protect "free trade and sailor's rights," and American rights on land.

I'll bet you know this part of the story. Soldiers, stationed at Fort McHenry, a star-shaped fort situated on a peninsula out in the middle of the harbor, successfully held off a British attack on Baltimore. This victory was witnessed by Francis Scott Key from the deck of a British cruiser. His commemorative poem is now our national anthem.

Since then Baltimore has experienced a number of setbacks and rebirths. A fire in 1900 burned down most of its business district, and the Depression took a big chunk out of a local economy that, unlike Washington, DC, didn't have a growing federal government to protect it. However, the city is in the midst of a major comeback.

The downtown area, once primarily dilapidated wharves and warehouses, now hosts some major family attractions, such as the National Aquarium in Baltimore, the Baltimore Orioles' stellar 'retro' baseball ball park at Camden Yards, the Maryland Science Center, and the Maritime Museum, all built around a renovated inner harbor enhanced by street entertainers, open-air concerts, fireworks, parades, paddle boats, cruise boats, an outdoor ice-skating rink, and major shopping and restaurants.

Baltimore

Charming historic neighborhoods surround the Inner Harbor, each offering their own character, history, and cuisine:

- **Fell's Point**, an upscale neighborhood of shops, art galleries, and choice restaurants (and at night a rocking little town with packed bars);

- **Pimlico:** The world-renowned home of the Preakness horse race;

- **Little Italy** (Yeah, that's right, Little Italy): With two bocce ball courts and a bunch of really good spaghetti joints, its people, events and good food make Little Italy a favorite destination for tourists and locals alike; and

- **Hampden**, home of the world's brightest and strangest Christmas light display.

Adam T. Lass

Baltimore's Washington Monument

I am particularly fond of Mount Vernon (*not* the same Mount Vernon as George Washington's home and final resting place outside Alexandria). The best address in town in the 1700s and 1800s, it has once again become the cultural center of the city, with the Peabody Conservatory of Music, the Walters Art Gallery; and the Basilica of the National Shrine of the Assumption, the first Roman Catholic cathedral in the United States, all clustered around Baltimore's own (and the nation's first, I might add) Washington monument in Mount Vernon Square.

All that said, however, our favorite things to do in Baltimore are taking in an Orioles game at Camden Yards and combining a walk around the Inner Harbor with a visit to the spectacular National Aquarium.

Also in the Neighborhood
- *BWI Airport*

Day Trips

Oriole Park at Camden Yards

333 West Camden Street
Baltimore, MD 21201
(410) 685-9800; tickets, (888) 848-BIRD (Ticketmaster);
tour tickets, (410) 547-6234
www.theorioles.com

Camden Yards

Tickets: $9-$40

Hours: Box office open in baseball
season Mon-Sat, 9 am - 5 pm;
Sun, noon - 5 p.m.

The park opened in early 1994 on the site of the former Camden railroad yards, but you would never believe it looking around from a seat in the bleachers behind third base. The Yards is a miracle of inspired architecture, traditional in look and intimate in feel as any of the long-gone and much-missed ball fields such as Brooklyn's Ebbets Field, and yet it is remarkably comfortable and sports modern conveniences (like enough bathrooms.)

Out front, you'll notice a statue of the town's local baseball hero, the Babe. He may have played in those other cities, but George Herman Ruth was born two blocks from the stadium, and his dad ran Ruth's Cafe on the ground floor of their house at Conway and Little Paca Street, now center field at Oriole Park. Now that's tradition.

National Aquarium (Baltimore)

Pier 3, 501 E Pratt Street
Baltimore, MD 21202
(410) 576-3800
www.aqua.org

National Aquarium (Baltimore)

Hours: March-June & Sept-Oct: Sat-Thurs. 9 am - 5 pm;
Fri, 9 am - 8 pm; July-Aug: Daily 9 am - 8 pm;
Nov-Feb: Sat-Thurs, 10 am - 5 pm; Fri, 10 am - 8 pm;
Dec 24, 10 am - 1 pm; Closed Thanksgiving, Dec 25.

Cost: General, $15; Seniors 62 and over, $12; Children
3-11, $8.50; Children under 3, free.

Sharks, electric eels, a giant Pacific octopus, dolphins and seals and sea-horses! More than 14,000 aquatic creatures in a million gallons of water!

But the most impressive thing in the National Aquarium in Baltimore may well be what you see when you first walk in: "Wings in the Water." Dozens of huge rays – sting rays, butterfly rays, cownose rays – swimming, soaring, and swooping in a 265,000-gallon pool. (There are usually a couple of sharks in the pool as well.) You can watch them from above, or go down a floor and see them at eye level behind glass, and either way, they're beautiful.

Baltimore

This is one of the largest aquariums on the East Coast – and one of the best anywhere. In addition to "Wings In the Water," the shark tank, a "please-touch" Discovery Cove for children, "Surviving Through Adaptation" (starring the electric eel and the octopus), and the marine mammal pavilion with dolphins and a (replica of a) humpback whale, there are exhibits on the Amazon River forest, a tropical rain forest, a coral reef, and the aquatic life of western Maryland.

The Aquarium is on the revived Baltimore piers, and there's good food and shopping nearby (a good thing, because the cafeteria is nothing to write home about). You'll want to spend at least a long morning here – that will give you time to see just about everything.

Edgar Allen Poe House

203 Amity Street
Baltimore, MD 21223
(410) 396-7932
www.eapoe.org

The gloomy little two-and-a-half-story brick cottage, complete with narrow rooms, warped floors and twisting staircases, is the childhood home of famed (or perhaps infamous?) poet and novelist Edgar Allen Poe, the inventor of the mystery, an early theorist on the short story, and the creator of some of the most perfect horror stories ever committed to paper.

Edgar Allen Poe House

Open April-July & Oct-Dec–
Wed-Sat, noon - 3:45 pm;
Aug-Sept – Sat, noon - 3:45 pm;
Closed Jan-Mar.

Cost: General, $3;
12 and under, $1.

Closed for renovation
through April 2002

If you choose to visit this shrine to the spooky, where it's believed he penned such classics as his "Ms. Found in a Bottle," you can see Poe's telescope and sextant, his traveling desk, and a full-sized color reproduction of the only known portrait of his wife, Virginia, done at her death in 1847. No skulls, no bodies in the walls, no secret basements that anyone's found . . . yet, but there is a set of Gustave Doré's 1884 illustrations for Poe's "The Raven" and a series of videos and other displays on Poe's life as an author and his death, including several of bottles of cognac (a strange gift from another Baltimore mystery, the "Poe Toaster," who leaves an annual bottle on Poe's grave at midnight on the anniversary of his death), and a reprint of the harsh obituary by Poe's former friend Rufus Wilmot Griswold.

Day Trips

What's Nearby

American Visionary Art Museum

800 Key Highway
Baltimore, MD 21230
(410) 244-1900
www.avam.org

Towering sculptures and a giant whirligig – this is a museum that cherishes the wildest and furthest-out. Children will enjoy its plaza even if you don't take time to go in.

> **American Visionary Art Museum**
>
> Hours: Tues-Sun (and Martin Luther King Jr.'s birthday), 10 am - 6 pm; Closed Thanksgiving and Dec 25.
>
> Cost: General, $6; Seniors and students, $4; Children under 4, free.

Babe Ruth Birthplace and Museum

216 Emory Street
Baltimore, MD 21230
(410) 727-1539
www.baberuthmuseum.com

The Babe's story in objects and memorabilia, exhibited in the house where he was born.

> **Babe Ruth Birthplace and Museum**
>
> Hours: Daily during baseball season, April-Oct, 10 am - 5 pm; until 7 pm on days of Orioles home games; Nov-March, 10 am - 4 pm; Closed Thanksgiving, Dec 25, New Year's Day.
>
> Cost: General, $6; Seniors, $4; Children 5-16, $3.

Baltimore Museum of Art

10 Art Museum Drive
Baltimore, MD 21218
(410) 396-7100
www.artbma.org

A major art museum, particularly famous for its Matisse collection.

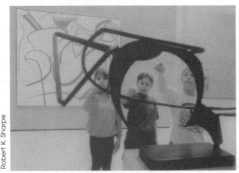

Robert K. Sharpe

Baltimore Museum of Art

> **Baltimore Museum of Art**
>
> Hours: Wed-Fri, 11 am - 5 pm; Sat-Sun, 11 am - 6 pm; 1st Thurs of the month until 9 pm; Closed July 4, Thanksgiving, Dec 25, New Year's Day.
>
> Cost: General (over 19), $6; Seniors and students with ID, $4; Children under 18, free.

Baltimore

Baltimore Museum of Industry

1415 Key Highway
Baltimore, MD 21230
(410) 727-4808

A hands-on museum of *things* – inventions, machines, etc. – that kids love to play with.

Baltimore Museum of Industry

Hours: Mon-Sat, 10 am - 5 pm; Sun, noon - 5 pm.

Cost: General, $6; Seniors and students, $4.50.

Baltimore Zoo

Druid Hill Park
Baltimore, MD 21217
(410) 366-5466
www.baltimorezoo.org

Baltimore Zoo

Hours: Daily, 10 am - 4 pm; extended summer hours.

Cost: General, $10; Seniors, $8; Children 2-11, $6 (but children under 12 admitted free 10 am - noon first Tuesday each month).

A medium-size (2,000 animals) zoo that can be seen in one day.

B & O Railroad Museum

901 W Pratt Street
Baltimore, MD 21223
(410) 752-2490
www.borail.org

B & O Railroad Museum

Hours: Daily, 10 am - 5 pm; Closed Easter, Thanksgiving, Dec 25, New Year's Eve & Day.

Cost: General, $8; Seniors, $7; Children, $5.

Affiliated with the Smithsonian Institution. Everything you wanted to know about America's old railroads.

Fort McHenry National Monument

Fort McHenry Park
Fort Avenue
Baltimore, MD

Fort McHenry National Monument

Hours: Daily, 8 am - 5 pm.

Cost: General, $5; Children 16 and under, free.

The place where Francis Scott Key saw "by the dawn's early light" that "our flag was still there."

Day Trips

Hard Rock Café

601 E Pratt Street
Baltimore, MD 21202
(410) 347-ROCK
www.hardrock.com

Baltimore's branch of the 'round-the-world theme restaurant is located on the Inner Harbor, making it convenient to several of the city's main attractions. And kids do love the Hard Rock.

Baltimore Harbor by the Hard Rock Café

National Lacrosse Museum

113 W University Pkwy
Baltimore, MD 21210
(410) 235-6882

National Lacrosse Museum
Hours: Mon-Sat, 10 am - 3 pm.
Cost: General, $3; Children, $2.

For serious lacrosse fans or players. And we should warn you, Marylanders are *very* serious lacrosse players.

Mountains and Seashore

For much of this book, we've focused on a fairly urban landscape, punctuated by many very pleasant parks. But what makes the Washington, DC area so different from most major metropolitan areas is how close it is to rolling farmland and genuine wilderness. In one hour from downtown DC, you can be standing on a mountaintop over looking the sumptuous Shenandoah Valley or leaning on a dock piling in Annapolis waiting to board a Chesapeake Bay-bound fishing boat for the day. Another 30 minutes, and you can see where John Brown martyred himself to abolitionism and then ride a raft over white-water rapids, or spend the day gunk-holing coves and prowling islands in rented sailboats or sea kayaks.

Here are two more day trips that will rival any outdoors experience in the country.

Harper's Ferry

Harper's Ferry, West Virginia

Harper's Ferry, West Virginia

It usually takes me about an hour and a half to make this 68-mile trip. Starting from the White House at 1600 Pennsylvania Ave. NW...

- Go north on 16th ST NW two blocks to K St. NW and turn left.
- Take K St. for about mile (it will become Water St.).
- This next part is basically a big right-hand circle to get you onto the Key Bridge. Turn right onto K ST NW/US-29 and then a slight right onto the Whitehurst Freeway/US-29 S, and then right again on M ST NW and then right again onto the bridge.
- Stay on the right as you cross the Potomac on the Key Bridge, and take the George Washington Memorial Parkway ramp towards Mclean/I-495/Maryland.
- Head up the Parkway about 7 _ miles to the Washington Beltway (designated I-495 in this stretch).
- Take the I-495 North exit towards Maryland. This will take you back across the Potomac. Get used to it. You'll be doing that a lot today.
- Take I-495 about four miles to Exit 38 for I-270 Rockville/Frederick (it's on the left).
- After about 3 miles, you'll merge with I-270 proper. This is a good thing. Stay on I-270 for about thirty miles. It will become US-40 W.
- Take the US-15 South/US-340 West exit.
- Take US-340 west about 19 miles, and then turn right onto Shenandoah St.
- Turn left onto High St. /US-340 Alt. and you're there.

Note that this route to I-270 is also how to get to the west side of the Washington Beltway, and any points you wish to reach from there.

Wedged snugly into the confluence of the Potomac and Shenandoah Rivers, the tiny village of Harper's Ferry seems like an unlikely spot for a revolution. Its steep cobbled streets, teetering Civil War-era buildings, and alpine vistas seem better suited for strolling or picnicking. But this bucolic West Virginia town (it was a Virginia town, of course, until Virginia seceded from the Union in 1861 and the western part of the state chose not to) did indeed play a pivotal historic role.

Around 1761, Philadelphia builder Robert Harper established ferry service across the Potomac making the new town a convenient marshaling and jump-off point for settlers heading west. The strategic value of that ferry was quickly grasped by the old surveyor himself, and when George Washington became President, he arranged to have one of the fledgling country's two arsenals located there.

Day Trips

The Harper's Ferry Arsenal became one our first military R&D centers and was well-known for its high-quality rifled muskets. Soon, the arsenal attracted other like-minded businesses such as the Hall Rifle Works, which popularized the concept of interchangeable parts to produce breech-loading rifles.

In 1833, the Chesapeake and Ohio Canal reached the ferry, connecting the town with markets in Washington, DC. And a year later, the Baltimore & Ohio Railroad followed, making Harper's an important stop on one the nation's three vital east-west rail links.

Abolitionist John Brown was the first of many armed parties to sweep through town. Actually, he didn't exactly sweep. On October 16, 1859, he and a small party seized the armory and arsenal for a couple of days figuring to use the guns to equip a private anti-slavery army. Their reward: those who weren't shot in the battle were hanged afterwards. The attempt wasn't the total failure it might have seemed to Brown. Word of the incident spread widely and is said by some to be one of the catalysts that triggered the Civil War. (A bit of trivia for you: The federal officer who commanded the operation to retake the arsenal from Brown was a West Point-trained U.S. Army colonel named Robert E. Lee.)

Over the next few years, Harper's strategic location was almost its demise, as various Union and Confederate generals sought to control the little town. After the war, the ferry was little more than a ghost town. The federal government sold what was left of the armory and arsenal and other property. Efforts to rebuild its commercial base were frequently devastated by record-breaking floods.

> **Harper's Ferry National Historical Park**
> Rte 340
> Harper's Ferry, WV
> (304) 535-6298

But history wasn't through with Harper's Ferry. In the 1890s, civil rights leaders convened at Storer College, a small, church-owned school for African-Americans, to create a new national organization to fight for the rights of blacks, a meeting that eventually lead to the birth of the NAACP.

And the railroad that had been such a pox during the war years became the savior of the upper town. By the turn of the century, 28 trains a day were arriving, full of tourists looking for a break from Washington's heat and humidity.

Harper's Ferry

By World War II, the federal government began to reclaim what it had abandoned, declaring the lower town a national monument now known as the Harper's Ferry National Historical Park.

You can still reach Harper's Ferry via a pleasant one-hour train ride up from Union Station, and it's a trip well worth taking. The historic township, with its tours, restored buildings and authentic eateries would be enough to fill anyone's day in the most satisfying fashion. But I promised you the great outdoors, and Harper's Ferry delivers – in a big way.

Harper's Ferry sits at the confluence of two great rivers, the Potomac and the Shenandoah. If you're into water sports, this is Nirvana. This town's got everything, from placid tubing and stellar fishing to major white water to challenge the most jaded adventurer. I cut my white-water canoeing teeth (and several other parts of my body) on the class-III (class-IV in heavy spring waters) run from "Bull Falls" to the "White Horse" and learned true boat mastery negotiating the mile-long rock garden known as the "Staircase" in August's calm.

Forgot to bring a boat of your own? Don't let that stop you. There are a plethora of guide services here that will get you all set up, whether you're just looking for an hour-long float and a picnic on the rocks or a major thrill ride on one of big rubber rafts. I've had particularly good luck with an outfit called River Riders.

River Riders

RR 5 Box 1260
Harper's Ferry, WV 25425
(800) 326-7238

River Riders is licensed by the West Virginia Division of Natural Resources and is staffed by world-class guides with the seasoned skills and know-how to provide you with the safest and most enjoyable trip possible.

Those who don't want to get wet can also rent bicycles for rides down the C&O Canal Tow Path.

Day Trips

Annapolis and the Chesapeake Bay

Annapolis and the Chesapeake Bay

This starts out exactly the same as the instructions for Baltimore. There will be a little zig-zagging in the beginning to get around one of Washington's endless squares. Stay the course and you'll get there just fine. Heading out from the White House at 1600 Pennsylvania Ave. NW...

- Start by heading east on H St. NW towards Madison Pl. NW.
- In about four blocks, bear left onto New York Ave NW.
- After another four blocks, you'll hit Mt. Vernon Square: bear right onto K St. NW. As you pass the square, K St. will magically turn into Massachusetts Ave NW. This is okay.
- Go one block on Massachusetts and then turn left onto 6th St NW/US-1/US-50.
- After two blocks, turn right onto New York Ave. NW/US-50. Congratulations: the hard part is over.
- After about four miles of industrial park hell, New York Ave. becomes a highway: US-50. Stay on it for about 26 miles.
- Take exit 24 onto MD-70/Rowe blvd. heading east (keep right at the fork in the ramp) 0.29 miles
- Take Rowe Blvd./MD-70 east about a mile and bear gently right and then merge onto Northwest St.
- Go around the Circle to Main St., which will take you directly to the City Dock.

For our last day trip, let's try a little something different. How about a major historical town, with lots of museums, shopping, and stellar water sports? Trust me, Harper's Ferry and Annapolis are different as night and day. While Harper's Ferry is a quaint little mountain hamlet, Annapolis is the Maryland state capital, Belle of the Chesapeake Bay, and home to the U.S. Naval Academy. It's still kind of quaint, but in a much grander sort of way.

Annapolis

Let's start by placing it in both its historical and geographical context. Geographically speaking, it's all about the bay (it's all about the bay from your kids' point view too, but I'll cover that in a moment). The Chesapeake Bay is the largest body of water in Maryland. It's about 200 miles long from Havre de Grace, Maryland, to Norfolk, Virginia, and 35 miles wide where the Potomac River runs in. For all that size, it's actually pretty shallow. Other than a few deep troughs, it averages about 21 feet in depth.

The Atlantic Beaches are only an hour from Annapolis and the Bay

It's part of the largest estuarial watershed in the United States – 64,000 square miles – and receives its fresh water from 150 major rivers and streams in Delaware, Maryland, New York, Pennsylvania, Virginia, West Virginia, and the District of Columbia. The other half of its 18 trillion gallons of water comes in from the Atlantic. That's what makes it an estuary: it's a mixing bowl of salt and fresh water. And that size and mixture of waters is what gives it such a fascinating mix of wildlife along its 11,684 miles of shoreline (more than the entire West Coast) with more than 3,600 species of plants, fish and animals, including 348 species of finfish, 173 species of shellfish, and more than 2,700 plant species. The Chesapeake is also a permanent home to 29 species of waterfowl and is a major resting ground along the Atlantic Migratory Bird Flyway, making it the winter home to *one million* waterfowl. The bay produces 500 million pounds of seafood per year.

There is evidence that Paleo-Indians were hunting mammoth, great bison, and caribou in these parts more than 10,000 years ago. By 1,000 B.C.E., Maryland was home to more than 8,000 Native Americans from about 40 different tribes.

Day Trips

I've heard it said that its name means "great salt water" or "great shellfish bay," but when pressed, historians will concede that they really don't do not know what the Native Americans called the bay. The name Chesapeake originates from "Chesepiuk," an Algonquian village near the mouth of the bay stumbled across by colonists from Roanoke in 1585. In 1608, Captain John Smith wrote that there was "no place more perfect for man's habitation."

In 1649, a small group of Virginia Puritans set up shop at the mouth of the Severn River. They originally named the fledgling town Providence, a nice pious, and totally impolitic idea. They soon caught on to how things really work and renamed it Anne Arundel Town to honor Lady Anne of Arundel, the wife of their sponsor, Cecil Calvert of Baltimore, Ireland. By 1695, it became the capital city of proprietary Maryland. The town was soon renamed again, this time to Annapolis in honor of Princess Anne, heir to the English throne.

Eighteenth-century Annapolis was a cultural and social hot spot. Celebrities like George Washington (he liked to play the horses at a track in nearby Parole, Maryland) and Thomas Jefferson could be seen strolling down the picturesque streets near the Annapolis harbor. Needless to say, downtown Annapolis is now a National Historic District, jam packed with classic Georgian mansions like the William Paca House, the Chase-Lloyd House, the Hammond-Harwood House, and the Charles Carroll House.

Annapolis is also a bit of a college town, with two pretty significant campuses. The country's third oldest college (and one of the first public schools in America) is St. John's College, where your kids can stand under the limbs of the 400-year-old Liberty Tree, a place that legend holds to be one of the secret meeting points of the revolutionary "Sons of Liberty."

And, of course, there's the school that's become synonymous with the town. Since 1845, the U.S. Naval Academy has insured Annapolis a place, not just on the local stage as a state capital, but on the world stage as well, as the source of the officers who command the most powerful navy in the history of the world.

One more history lesson and I'll get on to the fun stuff. Annapolis plays an important role in American history that is too often ignored. Head down to the city docks, and right there alongside "Ego Alley" (so named for the reeeeeally expensive power and sailboats that tie up daily), you'll see a plaque that is the first of a planned three-part memorial noting the arrival point in America of *Roots* author Alex Haley's ancestor, Kunte Kinte.

Annapolis

Annapolis is also home to the Banneker-Douglass Museum of Afro-American Life and History, Maryland's official repository of African-American history, located in the former Mt. Moriah Church. The museum offers rotating exhibits on the life and contributions of the area's African-American citizens.

The Historic Annapolis Foundation

77 Main Street
Annapolis, MD 21401
(410) 268-5576
www.annapolis.org

For more information on the history of Annapolis, the Historic Annapolis Foundation provides an audiotape tour recounting the history of African-Americans in Annapolis and a Three Centuries guided walking tour of significant sites in African-American history in Annapolis (led by costumed colonial guides!).

Now that your kids have been filled to the gills with that important historical stuff, we can move on to the real reason you want to come down this way, and that's to get out on the water and eat really good seafood.

While there are any number of available tour boats, I have particularly enjoyed my time aboard the *Woodwind II*. Owned and operated by two retired school teachers, Ken and Ellen Kaye, and their daughter Jennifer, both the

Woodwind II

Annapolis Marriott Hotel
80 Compromise Street
Annapolis, MD 21401
(410) 269-4213
www.schoonerwoodwind.com

Cost: General, $25-$29; seniors, $23-$27; children, $15 children

Woodwind and her sister ship the *Woodwind II* are beautiful 74-foot schooners that sail up to four times daily throughout the summer season from the Annapolis Marriott Waterfront Hotel. The rides are thrilling in a quiet sort of way, the views are spectacular, and the crews are competent and kind. They'll gently encourage your kids to join in hoisting sails and make sure that everyone gets some time at the wheel. This is real grade-A stuff you and your kids aren't likely to forget.

Captain Perry Davidson's Excalibur

11170 Meadow Ridge Road
Cordova, MD 21625
(410) 763-8899
www.excaliburcharters.com

Cost: $450/day for six people

If powerboats and fishing are more your speed, I can highly recommend chartering Captain Perry Davidson's *Excalibur*, a 1982 custom 42-foot fiberglass Chesapeake Bay-built charter boat. Perry was born and raised on the Eastern shore and has fished the Chesapeake Bay and its

Day Trips

tributaries since he was a young boy. He'll gladly take you out to a 'secret' spot or two for a day well spent fishing for spring trophy striped bass, spot, hardheads, white perch, blue fish, sea trout, fall rockfish stripe bass or for just plain old crabbing. (He steams the crabs right on board – now that's fresh!) Perry has a Maryland saltwater license, and provides all the bait and tackle you'll need. Just be sure to book well in advance. He books up quickly in the summer.

What's Nearby

Ballet Theatre of Annapolis

Maryland Hall for the Creative Arts
801 Chase Street
Annapolis, MD 21401
(410) 263-8289
www.btaballet.org

The largest professional ballet company in Maryland.

Banneker-Douglass Museum

84 Franklin Street
Annapolis, MD 21401
(410) 216-6180
www.marylandhistoricaltrust.net

The State of Maryland's official repository of Afrian-American culture, named for abolitionist and statesman Frederick Douglass and Revolutionary War engineer Benjamin Banneker. The museum's collection includes art, documents, and rare books.

Banneker-Douglass Museum

Hours: Tues-Fri, 10 am - 3 pm; Sat, noon - 4 pm.

Cost: Free.

Chesapeake Bay Maritime Museum

Mill Street
St. Michaels, MD 21663
mailing address:
PO Box 636
St. Michaels, MD 21663
(410) 745-2916
www.cbmm.org

Chesapeake Bay Maritime Museum

Hours: Summer – 9 am - 6 pm; Spring-Fall – 9 am - 4 pm; Winter, 9 am - 4pm; Closed Thanksgiving and Dec 25.

Cost: General, $7.50; Seniors, $6.50; Children 6-17, $3; under 6, free.

Visit a restored 1879 lighthouse, a fishing boat, and a working boatyard for a taste of Maryland's 19th-century seafaring life.

5 Appendix

Calendar of Festivals and Seasonal Events

Hunt for wooden "Easter eggs" on the White House lawn, watch Chinese dragons parade through downtown DC, revel in the beauty of 3,000 blooming cherry trees, or watch a 16th-century jousting contest; some of Washington's annual events are world-famous, others are secrets you can find out only from DC insiders. Here's a highly selective list of some of the city's parades, festivals, and celebrations (many of them are annual events for our family). Before you go, however, you might call, write, or look up the Washington, DC, Convention and Visitors Bureau, 1212 New York Ave. NW, #600, Washington, DC 20005, 202/789-7000, **www.washington.org**, for more festivities going on during your visit.

January

January 19 (and/or nearest Monday): **Martin Luther King Jr. birthday**. Dr. King's birthday is the occasion for a broad range of political and cultural events in Washington. The Martin Luther King, Jr. Memorial Library is the site for many and can provide information about others. 901 G St. NW, Washington, DC 20001; 202/727-1111; **www.dclibrary.org/mlk**.

January-February

Late January-early February: **Chinese New Year**. The annual parade, dragons and all, starts near the Chinatown Gateway Arch. Check the *Washington Post* for the date for your trip.

March

March 17 or nearest Sunday: **St. Patrick's Day Parade**. Washington's version of every town's celebration of all things Irish, from bagpipes to pubs. Constitution Avenue from 7th to 17th Sts. NW. (212) 637-2474, **www.dcstpatsparade.com**.

March-April

Easter Monday: **White House Easter Egg Roll**. One of Washington's most famous events, a huge party for children (age 3-6 and their adult companions) with entertainment and a wooden-egg hunt on the White House South Lawn. NOTE: The event was cancelled in 2002; call (202) 456-2200 to check.

Easter Monday: **African-American Family Day at the National Zoo**. The special annual celebration, held since 1889. Music, dance, and food. National Zoological Park, 3001 Connecticut Ave. NW, Washington, DC 20008, 202/357-2700, **www.si.edu/natzoo**. Admission free.

Appendix

End of March-Beginning of April: **Cherry Blossom Festival**. The other thing Washington is famous for: the spectacular blooming of 3,000 cherry trees given by the city of Tokyo to the people of Washington in 1912. Tidal Basin, (202) 547-1500, **www.nationalcherry-blossomfestival.org**

April

Opening Day at Camden Yard. You have to go to Baltimore for this, but it's worth it: the opening of the baseball season at Oriole Park-Camden Yard. 333 West Camden St., Baltimore, MD 21201; 410/685-9800; **www.theorioles.com**.

June

Shakespeare Free for All. Two weeks of free Shakespeare performances at the Carter Barron Amphitheater, 4850 Colorado Avenue NW at 16th St. (in Rock Creek Park), Washington, DC 20011, (202) 426-6837.

June 8-9, 2002: **Potomac Celtic Festival**. A tradition in our family, celebrating the Celtic cultures of the British Isles, Spain, and France with music, dance, historical re-enactments, and more. Morven Park's International Equestrian Center, Leesburg, VA; (800) 752-6118; **www.potomaccelticfest.org**. Cost: $15 general, $7 children, free for children under 6.

June-August, 2002

Jacqueline Kennedy's Washington. Nearly 60 performances, exhibits, walking tours, and other events, centered around the Corcoran Gallery's exhibition, "Jacqueline Kennedy: The White House Years." Special hotel packages available. For general information, call (212) 789-7000; for package deals, (800) 769-1212, ext. 17.

Late June-early July

The week (or so) before July 4: **The Smithsonian Festival of American Folk Life**. Music, of course, but also crafts, food, and lots of special events for kids. Along the Mall and elsewhere in the city; call the Smithsonian, (202) 357-2700 for details.

July

July 4: **Independence Day**. An all-day celebration, starting with an organ recital at the National Cathedral, followed by a very big parade down (where else?) Constitution Avenue, a free concert by the National Symphony Orchestra on the Capitol grounds, and fireworks near the Washington Monument. Check the *Washington Post* for details.

Calendar

August

August 9-17, 2002: **Montgomery County Agricultural Fair.** An old-fashioned country fair, mixing prize animals and midway games and rides. Gaithersburg, MD, **www.mcagfair.com**. Cost: "Pre-fair days" August 9-10, $3 general (not including rides), free for children under 7, parking $2; "fair days," August 11-17, $6 general.

August 31: **DC Blues Festival.** Great blues under the stars at the Carter Barron Amphitheatre (see Shakespeare Free for All in June for more information).

August-September-October

Weekends in all three months: **Maryland Renaissance Festival.** An annual entry in our family's calendar since its inception as a ratty traveling medieval carnival in 1977. Now permanently in a beautiful recreation of a 16th century English village, with craft and food booths, pubs, eight stages, a jousting arena and lots of games. If you stop at the Dancing Pig, tell them Adam sent you. Crownsville Rd., Crownsville, MD (just outside Annapolis); **www.rennfest.com**. Cost: $16 general, $14 seniors, $7 children 7-15, free for children 6 and under.

September

September 21-22, 2002: **Takoma Park Folk Festival.** A 25-year tradition in Takoma Park, with a wide range of folk music and other activities, including special events for children. Takoma Park Middle School, 7611 Piney Branch Rd., Takoma Park, MD 20910; for information, see **www.tpff.org**.

October

Columbus Day weekend: **Taste of DC.** A large number of Washington restaurants come out onto the streets, offering food (and entertainment) for the whole family along Pennsylvania Avenue between 7th and 14th Sts. NW. **www.washington.org/taste**

Columbus Day Weekend: **The National Latin-American Festival.** Food pavilions and a parade celebrate Washington's and the nation's Latino heritage. Constitution Avenue from the Washington Monument to the Capitol; **www.dclatino.com**.

December

Mid-month: **National Christmas Tree lighting.** Accompanied by choruses of Christmas carols, the President pushes the button that lights one of the country's most spectacular Christmas trees. On the Ellipse; call (202) 619-7222 or check the *Washington Post* for details.

Index

Index

Index

Index

Index

Washington DC Metro System Map

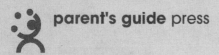
parent's guide press

Good For You.
Good For Your Kids.

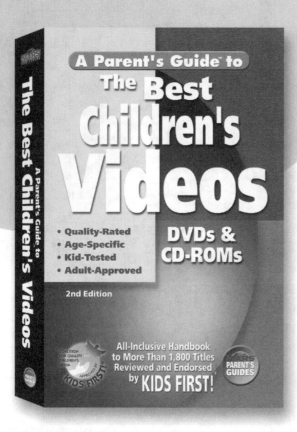

A Parent's Guide to THE BEST CHILDREN'S VIDEOS
Second Edition. Formerly *The New York Times Guide to the Best Children's Videos*, 0671036696.

ISBN 1-931199-04-3
$19.95 (Sep 2001)
495 Pages —Trade Paperback—**Available in Library Bindings**
Cross-referenced index, numerous b/w photos.

"This volume (is) essential as a ready-reference for parents and for any library seeking to provide high-caliber and unobjectionable children's media to their patrons. Recommended for all public libraries."

- Library Journal

A Parent's Guide to
SCHOOL PROJECTS
ISBN 1-931199-08-6
$17.95 (May 2002)
216 pages—Trade Paperback
Available in Library Bindings
Index, 30 b/w Photos

The only book about the latest trend in Elementary and Middle School Education.

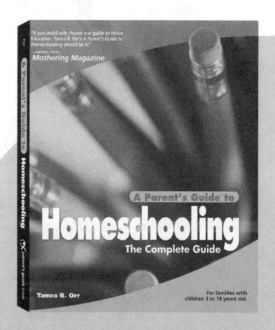

Written by Tamra B. Orr, author of 101 Ways to Make Your Library Homeschooling Friendly and 125 Things Homeschoolers Can Do on the Internet.

A Parent's Guide to
HOMESCHOOLING
ISBN 1-931199-09-4
$22.95 (June 2002)
336 pages—Trade Paperback
Available in Library Bindings
Bibliography, Index, 10 Illustrations